Stumbling Naked in the Dark™:
Overcoming Mistakes Men Make With Women

By
Bradley Fenton

Simon & Brown
www.simonandbrown.com

ISBN-13: 978-0-9814843-3-4
ISBN-10: 0-9814843-3-6

Library of Congress Control Number: 2008903660
Library of Congress subject headings:
Dating (social customs)
Mate selections
Single women – Psychology
Single men – Psychology

1.2

Author Online! To contact Bradley, please write to
fentonbm@yahoo.com

Kim, Carey, Sep and Kirby,

Thank You!

Chapters

1

State of the "Union"

Guys, who taught you how to interact with women?

Until now, we men have had no clear source from which to gain factual and valid information on which practices bring about the best results with women. Information on the subject is confusing and fragmented at best. It is often based on the well-meaning advice of family members and friends who speak from emotions based on their own personal experiences, which may or may not be useful.

Although dealing with women is a topic of vital importance, there are not many places for men to gain crucial information about it, other than confusing bits and pieces contained within magazines, television, and movies. Thousands of columns are published yearly in men's journals such as *Maxim* and *GQ*, exclaiming, "100 Tips That Drive Women Crazy!" While these articles are somewhat entertaining, they are often illogical and useless when it comes to real-life situations, and they're usually based on the advice of personal friends and associates of their respective authors instead of any kind of credible authority.

Movies and television also play a significant yet confusing role in how we think we should act around women. Like it or not, actors such as Robert De Niro, Al Pacino, Jack Nicholson, Steve McQueen and Vince Vaughn are among those whose roles -- and sometimes personal lives -- have set a cultural benchmark on how we believe men should act and be perceived. After we watch their performances, we are left with the Big Question: What is it about these actors that is so attractive to women? We wonder how we can replicate it ourselves. Is the recipe to attraction simply good looks, fame and fortune? Or are there some other ingredients? Unfortunately, we're left to figure it out on our own.

The hard truth is this: Our culture teaches men skills and tactics that are actually harmful to our success with women.

It is our hope that when you've finished this book, you may be able to resolve most of the confusion you feel about this subject. You'll understand what makes men attractive to women, and you'll be able to put this into action in your own life in a constructive, satisfying way.

Now more than ever, men need to gain a better understanding of what women want, and they need to develop the ability to deliver it to them. We need this information because many men are in a very serious predicament, one that often goes unspoken. Tens of thousands of sharp and talented men are stumbling naked in the dark. It's what I call men who are not getting their needs met. Love, sex and tactile needs are basic requirements we have as human beings but in today's fast-paced society, they often seem elusive. Many men go for months at a time without having a date, let alone having their physical needs satisfied. This unfortunate trend is a fast-growing one, contributed to by such factors as longer work hours and an increase in the average age at which men marry. This problem affects not only a lot of lonely and frustrated men but women as well.

To add to this already very stressful problem, the simple act of asking for help in dealing with women is seen as proof that a man is weak or has a character flaw. Somewhere inside us, we know there must be better information out there but we feel we must be covert about attaining it so that we're not considered unmanly.

Until now, men frustrated with their social lives have had two options. One is to continue struggling along by themselves and hope things turn around. The other is to turn to the privacy and safety of professional psychiatric help to find some relief and guidance. The reason many men take this second option is that they are suffering from the basic problem of having *trouble getting what they want* – the confidence it takes to have repeated successful interactions with women and therefore the opportunity to have a relationship with a woman they truly choose to be with -- because nobody ever taught them how to do it in an effective manner that produces optimum results. This problem is often the root cause of seemingly endless social and emotional turmoil for men.

If you have been frustrated with your dating life you are certainly reading the right book.

Powerful Men

Our culture commonly equates power with the capacity one has to control money and/or people. Give yourself a few seconds and think of a powerful man. Most people tend to think of a successful businessman or politician such as Bill Gates or Bill Clinton, a famous entertainer like Tom Cruise or Steven Spielberg, or a professional athlete like Michael Jordan or Tiger Woods. Many men daydream about what it would be like to have that kind of power, even for just one day. What would it be like to have enormous amounts of money, the finest toys at your disposal and the opportunity to meet thousands of beautiful and willing women?

The fact is most men will never be able to command that sort of power. And many others aren't even interested in it in the first place. Regardless, most men do want to be powerful in their own environments. That may mean the ability to function more productively during interactions with women at our local hang-outs, or improving at work or school. Whatever our specific desires, we want the ability to do the best we can for ourselves while enjoying and hopefully repeating those positive experiences.

For men, interactions with women in today's social settings are often burdened with pressure and distrust, not to mention that these interactions frequently end with an unfavorable result. Failure with women causes a vicious cycle of repeated failure, creating much anxiety and hopelessness.

The ability for men to create and repeat more favorable results while interacting with women leads to an increased feeling of empowerment. You will learn in this book to better understand the dynamics of what really takes place during your interactions with women. This will equip you with the tools to begin making positive changes. If you think about it, the "edge" that the aforementioned titans of industry and popular culture have over the general population of men is that they have significantly better odds with women due to more options and opportunities via their notoriety, access to money and extravagant assets. Since they have more opportunities to meet women and are considered very attractive, they have a greater likelihood that their interactions will be successful.

Guess what? You can increase your options and opportunities -- and your likelihood of success with women -- without having to become rich and famous. One of the goals of this book is to greatly increase your odds of succeeding with women by changing your mindset and your behavior. This, in turn, will afford you new benefits in your social life.

By expanding your self-awareness and realizing what you are really capable of carrying out while dating and interacting with women, you can increase your choices about how to succeed. And you can do it in a way that is beneficial to both you and the woman you are with. You may find that you're a lot more powerful than you now realize.

As you read through this book, use your intellect and common sense to ask yourself questions as to when this material would or would not make sense for you to apply in your own life. Feel free to analyze and question everything.

The "Superman Myth"

I want to debunk a myth for you now that must be dealt with up front. It's called the "Superman Myth." It's the myth of a man who from birth naturally succeeds with women. The truth is, success with women is not an innate skill that only a select few men possess. *We all have access to this skill -- it's a matter of breaking down mental blocks to get to it and benefit from it.*

There is a misperception that some men are born with a 'gift of gab' for interacting with women, or that they are irresistible to women, and this inborn skill is the only sure route to success. That is a falsehood. *Men do not have to be born this way; we can learn to become this way by tapping into what we already possess naturally.* Let me explain.

Some men learn from experience very early on in their lives that a certain way of dealing with women elicits the response they desire. Unaware of what they are doing, they continue to do what they have always done because they have been pleased with the results. Think of these men as the friends you may know that have an amazing "way" with women. They may not have been that much better-looking than other men but they possessed a certain undefined "something" that women were attracted to. Basically, whatever it is they did worked and got results.

On the other hand, some men who have had less success with women are often equally unaware of their practices. Unfortunately, like their successful counterparts, these men continue to do what they have always done in the past – but are continually disappointed and unfulfilled. For some of these less-contented men there comes a point when they realize the need to make a change. Often through the anguish of yet another frustrating interaction or experience, they realize that other men are getting better results with women then they are. It's upsetting.

If the way you interact with women is truly getting you the results you want, then this book is not for you. While it can drastically increase your success rate with women, know that there is not one perfect dating methodology or strategy that works in every situation all the time. While this book provides a truly beautiful framework that is a continual work-in-progress, there are many styles that work. If everything is going well with your social life, keep doing whatever it is you're doing and I wish you continued success.

If your interactions with women are not going as smoothly as you want and are often frustrating, then I have good news. I have pinpointed the reasons why men succeed with women and organized these concepts into a mental training method. If you are open-minded to the fact there may be a better way, please read on. I can guarantee that what is here will be, at minimum, thought-provoking if not extremely worthwhile.

2
What's Going On?

I would like to define two words for you as they appear in *Webster's Dictionary.*

Confidence - (1) "a state of trust" or (2) "reliance, a feeling of hope on which one relies" or (3) "self-reliance."

And...

Confidence Game - "a swindling by winning someone's trust and then defrauding her." **(The Webster's definition says, 'defrauding him.' But for our purposes, I use the word 'her.')

It's amazing what happens when the word "confidence" is followed by the word "game." It changes the entire meaning of "confidence" from a positive into a negative. The same is true for what many men do in the world of dating. By playing dating "games," we create a negative dynamic. Since we created it, the burden falls on us to fix it.

With sex as the trophy, generations of men have pursued women. The fact that men have historically pursued sex as the main goal of dating and interacting with women has resulted in relationships beginning with an adversarial dynamic. In other words, dating becomes a game in which someone wins and someone loses. This is exemplified by the negative stigma that men are always trying to do something "to" women rather than to "be with" them. It generates the common slang word "player" – which is not complimentary -- and results in a negative perception of women towards men and vice versa.

From the female perspective, women become fearful that they will be pressured into doing something that they will regret or is not the right thing for them to do. At the same time, we men are concerned that if we do something wrong or don't act right, we will lose by not getting our needs met. There will be no sex or love for us.

For men, this adversarial thinking breeds the absurd but deeply instilled idea that men who are successful with women should be able to triumph over any problem or obstacle leading to sex, including a disparity between our needs, values and beliefs and the needs, values and beliefs of the woman we are with. *It is mind-boggling how many men mistakenly believe that they have done something wrong if a woman chooses not to go out with them or become intimate with them.* Since many men are unknowingly approaching relationships with women as a game, they feel the pressure of losing if they don't get what they want.

In this win-lose adversarial relationship, both men and women engage in destructive behavior that makes dating difficult right from the first interaction.

Men's Common Negative Behaviors That Make Dating More Difficult

- Men don't listen to women.
- Men make guesses about women.
- Men have inflexible solutions to women's problems.

- Men feel it will take too long to become intimate or get into a relationship with a certain woman.
- Men desperately need to have sex.
- Men don't understand the women they are dating.
- Men feel they know what women need more than they do.

Women's Common Negative Behaviors That Make Dating More Difficult

- Women don't know what they need from men.
- Women can't or won't verbalize what they need from men.
- Women don't see eye to eye on what they need from men.
- Women will not give good information to men.
- Women are unrealistic about the time it takes to form a committed relationship or to become intimate with men.
- Women procrastinate and can't or won't make decisions about relationships with men.

If the relationship has these problems early on, they tend to compound because, eventually, at least one of the parties is not getting his or her needs met. Not getting needs met leads to the following most common problems:

Men Who Don't Get Their Needs Met

- Become resentful and then become more aggressive and turn up the pressure on women.
- Turn their resentment inward and lose their self-confidence and assertiveness. Their needs come second to the woman's and they become "whipped."

- Many may turn their resentment outward and blame external factors such as the way they look, their financial status or their job.

Women Who Don't Get Their Needs Met

- Become distant and don't return phone calls.
- Drag out decisions because they don't feel comfortable making them in the first place.
- Keep their guard up and don't share information about what they need.
- Some may subordinate themselves and their needs, leading to abusive relationships.
- May begin dating other men without expressing their unhappiness about their relationship with you.

Know that in adversarial or game-like relationships, losers resent winners. And in games, there is usually a winner and a loser. In this situation, one person will always be upset with the other. Even in games where there is good sportsmanship, are you really happy when the other team wins and your team loses? No, you're bitter that the other team won, aren't you? People react in a similar fashion when it comes to relationships. Both men and women cultivate their own ways of achieving domination, all of which impede the stream of communication and also maintain the adversarial characteristics of the relationship.

What's happening is that a power struggle is taking place beneath the surface of the relationship. When men pursue sex as a trophy, like we do nearly all of the time, we not only initiate an adversarial dynamic but often act against our own best interests by becoming too aggressive. I call this being "aggressively flawed." And it's a big mistake – because the woman's response is to withdraw. It's a way of exerting negative power and control to get what we want -- and it is wrong and unfair to the woman. And, possibly more importantly to you, it doesn't work! It isn't nearly the best way to get your needs met in the first place! It is natural to want to have sex and relationships with women you find attractive. Unfortunately, the way most of us go about it is not only ludicrous but also exhausting and usually fruitless.

For athletes, being aggressively flawed can sometimes be a very good characteristic - especially if the sport closely resembles basic animalistic behavior. It can take a player to another level of force and attack, often leading to victory. Let's take Mike Tyson as an extreme case of an aggressively flawed individual. Within a controlled sporting environment like boxing (with the exception of his ear-biting fiasco), being overly aggressive has served Tyson very well during his illustrious boxing career. Unfortunately, we all know his negative aggression has not served him well in his social life and has caused him both personal and legal problems.

For men seeking women, being aggressively flawed often results in inappropriate behavior. Men confuse aggression with assertive action-taking, but they are very different. Aggression stifles the ability to establish trust, and trust is essential so that open and honest communication can take place with a woman. When either gender senses that they are being controlled or dominated, we resort to natural defense mechanisms to try to reassert our own power. In the typical win-lose game, these defense mechanisms include fight, flight or submit.

Fight -- fighting back openly or finding some way to get back at the other person;
Flight -- abandoning the relationship, either emotionally or physically;
Submit – giving in to the other person, thereby damaging one's own needs.

These defense mechanisms are the root cause of nearly all of the major interpersonal arguments and problems that men and women experience during relationships (who has decision-making control, financial control, etc.).   So why do we start the problem in the first place, by setting up an adversarial dynamic?

The answer is, *many men experience a perceived powerlessness when interacting with women.* The fact that getting our needs met is at stake makes for a very tense situation. If you have not had sex for months at a time, you understand just how tense it can be. You walk into a situation where there are attractive women and your animal instincts kick in. You want to feed your sexual craving but intellectually you may not know where to start. Your emotional and sexual needs are dependent on how well you can perform in your intellectual interactions. This creates a conflict between your logic and reasoning skills, on the one hand, and your animal instincts. This conflict makes interacting with women even more pressure-packed and stressful. Unfortunately, animal instincts usually prevail, which means you act emotionally aggressive, whether in active or passive ways.

In pressure-packed situations, we usually revert to what we have learned to do in the past. If your past experience has taught you to push, lie, wing it, do or say just about anything to get your needs met, or to avoid the interaction altogether, that's just what you will do over and over again. *The fact that there are no structures or guidelines to follow during our interactions with women always makes it an extremely unpredictable and stressful event.* It is such an exhausting process that many men avoid it altogether. They are described as shy or unsociable, when very often they simply feel uncomfortable playing the dating game. So they respectfully abstain from interacting, only to realize that the problem is still there waiting for us; we need to get our needs met. No wonder millions of Americans are on Prozac. It's depressing.

We live in a fast-food culture, and much of our society is based on instant gratification. The fact that men are not getting major needs like physical closeness and sex met for months or years at a time has given way to the enormous "quick-fix" pornography industry, which only perpetuates aggressive behavior. Why do we do this to ourselves?

Again, the problem stems from a perceived powerlessness that we men feel. It's the feeling of being a deer in headlights when you meet a woman to whom you are very attracted. It's often mistaken with having a "love at first sight" encounter. Let me be the first to say that the perceived powerlessness we feel is very real. And the reason is that women have developed a powerful system that they use when interacting with men. It may be a tough pill to swallow but women are significantly more powerful than we are in dating situations. This is due to their advanced emotional intelligence. Women have developed a natural defense mechanism for men, which they often use. And it's always the same system. Their system is more impressive and effective than the system -- or lack thereof -- that men use. It's the equivalent to playing a game or fighting a war in which women are armed with automatic weapons while we men are fighting with sticks and stones.

The sex craving we have is normal and natural but the ways many men go about obtaining sex creates a massive imbalance in power – with the woman having the power (however neither men nor women are generally aware of this). Let's learn about how women have developed a "guard" or system to deal with the dysfunctional practices of men.

Whether you are aware of it, there are always two dynamics or systems clashing heads when you interact with women: The Woman's System and the Man's System.

The Man's System

> 1. Do or say anything possible to have sex.
>   Period. That's it.

The Woman's System: Protecting Herself

> 1. Women may choose to be misleading to
> men. Women mislead men all the time to protect
> themselves. They believe that men will lie or say
> just about anything to have sex. And, for the
> most part, they are right. So, to defend against
> this, some women choose to mislead instead of
> being honest about their feelings. Two of the
> biggest misleading statements a woman makes
> appear during the first attempt a man makes at
> a potential relationship. The woman will say
> some form of, "I am interested in going out with
> you," when she doesn't mean it. Or, she will say
> some version of, "I am not interested in going out
> with you," when she may mean just the opposite.
> Women don't lie and mislead because they are
> bad, deceptive people; it's a defense mechanism.
> Unless a mutual friend introduced you to her,
> she doesn't know who you are and doesn't really
> know anything about you yet. There are twisted
> and aggressively flawed guys strolling around all
> over the world and she is smart to be careful.
> For all you know she just broke up with such a
> guy right before she met you. No wonder her
> defenses are up.

*Bob and Jane met at the party of a mutual friend.
After a nice conversation, Jane mentioned to Bob
that things were "over" with her long-term*

boyfriend. She went on to say, "I would like to start dating other guys like you to see what else is out there." Flattered, at the end of the night Bob approached Jane and said, " I enjoyed talking with you. Would you like to get together sometime?" Jane said, "I would like that." The two exchanged numbers. After a few unreturned voicemail messages, Bob felt really upset because Jane didn't call him back and began wondering what it was about him that made her not call back. Curious, Bob inquired to the mutual friend who had the party, Marc, about what had happened with Jane. Marc thought to himself for a while and then said, " I think a day before the party she found out her boyfriend was cheating on her and she was hurt. I think she still loves him though and they are trying to work everything out." Bob remembered distinctly when Jane said at the party that things "were over" with her and her boyfriend. Bob thought to himself, "I guess my interpretation of 'over' differed from hers." It was another case of things not always being what they seemed.

2. Women want to know if you're the right one for them. But if you're not, they won't tell you. Women want to know if you're a good match for them, which is just as it should be. And they vary in the time it takes them to reach this conclusion. But if you are not a good match, women won't tell you that because they don't want to hurt your feelings or feel like they're being mean. So what happens next?

3. Women don't answer the phone and won't return your messages. Let's say a woman has decided she's not interested in you or that your relationship is over but you don't know it yet. She simply stops taking your phone calls.

Meanwhile, you're taught that as a man, you should keep going, keep trying and keep pushing. Many men seem to actually like this abuse. It's very masochistic and many men get stuck on Step Three for weeks at a time. They end up becoming stressed out and lose sleep.

Jim had what he thought was an amazing first date with Mary. She told him she had a great time right before the two kissed goodnight. In fact, Mary even left Jim a phone message the following day saying that she "really had fun and thank you again." Jim was on cloud nine! He really thought she was a great girl with lots of potential. After a couple days had passed, Jim called Mary and thought it odd that she abruptly got off the phone with him exclaiming, "I have got to run -- can I call you back?" But she never did. A few more days passed and Jim left a couple more phone messages for Mary. Again, no return calls. After two weeks had passed with no returned phone calls, a million reasons ran through Jim's mind on what had happened with Mary. Most of them centered around what he must have done wrong. He couldn't pinpoint what went wrong. Jim had trouble believing that a woman would kiss him good-night and call him the next day to say thank you for a wonderful evening yet have her own reasons for thinking the two were not a good match.

4. Women exert the aggressive and ubiquitous line, "I want to slow things down," or "Let's take a break." Women exercise this option whenever they feel vulnerable, afraid or they have lost control of the relationship. It's a last-ditch effort to have an adversarial power shift. But lines such as these mean the relationship is

over -- because agreeing to them means the relationship cannot be balanced. Good relationships move forwards, not backwards. The only way for a relationship to move backwards is at someone's expense, and it's usually the man's.

Jason had been dating Pam for a little over two months when the two started becoming intimate. Jason truly cared for Pam and called her to make plans for the upcoming weekend. Pam asked Jason if he had a minute to talk. She went on to explain that she felt that things were moving "too fast" and they needed to "slow things down" because she "needed more time" to herself and maybe the two "should date some other people." Confused, Jason agreed and said, "If that's what you want, that's okay." He also told Pam he really cared about her and to take her time, and asked when could he next see her? Pam replied, "I think that I want to hang out with my friends this weekend and I will call you next week and tell you when a good time would be." The next week, Pam calls Jason on a Wednesday and the two make plans for that Saturday night. They went to dinner and a movie, and Jason kissed Pam goodnight. Pam didn't invite Jason into her apartment as she'd done every time on their previous twenty dates. Jason, bewildered, said, "I can't come up?" Pam said, "I need more time, everything is moving so fast." She then said goodnight. On the car ride home, Jason wondered things like: "How long is this going to last? What made Pam act so distant and stop us becoming intimate? Why do I feel uncomfortable and awkward the way things are now? Why do I get frustrated when I think about the situation with Pam?

In a dating relationship that is adversarial, the woman will win a vast majority of the time. Her system will reveal men who do not have her best intentions at heart, which is actually a very good thing for her. Unfortunately, her defense mechanisms will also eliminate many men who could be a good match for her but who are simply missing the tools to break through her defense system. So very often dating ends up not a win-lose situation, but instead a lose-lose scenario.

Because we lack a good system for dealing with women, men unknowingly default to the women's system, which means we lose most of the time. The reason is because of the different agendas between men and women -- men want sex while women want to find a trustworthy mate who understands her and accepts her how she is (a good match.) And of these two agendas, the woman's agenda is naturally more intuitive.

Lisa was set up with Fred for a blind date. Naturally, Fred followed the Man's System, while Lisa stuck with the Woman's System. When the two met, Fred started noticeably gawking at Lisa's body, especially her breasts, since sex was certainly first on his agenda—he wanted the sex trophy. Lisa noticed it. Nonetheless, the two continued on with their systems and the date. Fred's internal voice said to him, "Wow, I would love to see her naked." His internal voice had nothing to block it out, such as another agenda to focus on. With the sex trophy the primary goal on Fred's mind, he acted unnatural and awkward. Lisa realized this. She knew that Fred was not focused on finding a good match for himself or for Lisa. Therefore, he had no filter on his comments, he asked very few, if any, questions and he was unaware of the effect his communication was having on her. As we learned before, the first thing on Lisa's mind was whether Fred was a good match for her. Women can easily tell when men cannot detach themselves from the sex/ego block in their verbal and nonverbal behavior. Lisa wondered how Fred could be a good fit for her if he was so hypnotized by her chest that he could not take the time to listen to her in order to understand her better. Lisa determined quickly that Fred was a bad match.

So men, by going for the sex trophy, we are setting ourselves up to lose most of the time. We lose so often, in fact, that when we finally win, we are so ecstatic it's sad. Ever call up your friend at 3 a.m. to tell him you just had sex? An interaction has finally gone our way and we got our sexual needs taken care of so we want to shout it from the rooftops. This should be happening on a regular basis, but most often it's not. So we feel empowered for a small bit of time. But then soon enough we come down from our bliss and are into another six-month drought. A frustrating cycle indeed. For everyone's best interest, this desperation has to end.

3
What Do We Do Now?

Now that we know women have a more powerful system then we do, what next?

It's time to disengage and give up the "game." A change is needed in the way men perceive dating and interacting with women, which for   the vast majority of men, is just not working that well. In the previous chapter, we recognized the downsides and limitations of why it's not working when we explored the   existing   "game-like"   adversarial   model.   The following chapters provide an overview of how to break out of the adversarial model with new thinking and behavior while developing new, unorthodox skills to aid in the metamorphosis. These skills will aid you in getting your needs met in a way that exceeds even the best of game players.

You will learn a powerful framework that allows you to disengage from the dating game by becoming more   assertive,   direct   and   honest.   Rather   than abstaining from dating or being aggressive, this is a more intuitive way of interacting. Most importantly, it's much more effective than playing games, and certainly more rewarding and fun. And get this: You can always be yourself and you NEVER have to lie to women.

Our goal is to level the dynamic between males and females so we can interact fairly and in a way that maximizes the best outcome for everyone. Men must be able to take responsibility for causing the imbalance and then neutralize it. At first, as we do this, a majority of women will confuse our assertiveness, directness and honesty as gamesmanship and will continue to defend and protect themselves from the adversarial hazards they have grown accustomed to. That's all right. This system is designed to bring down the female guard in a way that benefits both men and women. The payoffs are tremendous: more intimacy, love and an increased sense of well-being.

We must understand that the main reason men fail with women is because we often lack the education and self-awareness to gauge the effects that our behavior is having on our interactions. We also have very little self-control during these dates and exchanges.

The reality of mate selection is that women are very attracted to men who are able to get what they want. It goes back to primal hunting and gathering times. If a woman were to have a mate roaming around the Serengeti for food, she would certainly want a man who would come home with dinner. It was an issue of survival.

What kind of man would consistently be able to provide food? A man who was skilled at manipulating his environment and educated as well as in tune with animal behavior, thereby allowing him to assertively and repeatedly make his kill. Other men hunted by going out and "hoping they got lucky." If your sustenance and survival were at stake, wouldn't you want to be hunting with someone who knew what he was doing rather than someone who was hoping to get lucky?

Like their primal ancestors, women continue to be attracted to men who get what they want. A man who is genuinely skilled at getting what he wants is usually capable of subconsciously or consciously manipulating his environment for favorable results.

Although the word manipulation is viewed in a negative context in our society, it is not always a bad thing. Like it or not, manipulation is occurring all around us every day of our lives. Healthy women are most attracted to certain characteristics exemplified in confident men, men who understand how to get what they want without violating a woman's autonomy. These are men who understand that *you cannot control women, you can only control yourself.*

The good news is you can get what you want – that is, be attractive to women – without lying or being manipulative in a negative way. It's all about self-confidence. And developing that is easier than you think.

The bottom line is that the more intuitive you become at getting what you want, the more influential you become with women. It's an emotional power that is practiced by men who are assertive. You will learn this assertiveness and why exactly it works so well with women, which will give you such an advantage over other single men that sometimes people will describe the results as unfair. You will learn how to get what you want with women without being harshly controlling, without being subservient and without forfeiting your self-esteem. And you never have to lie. In addition, you will have a deeper understanding of what women want. While not every woman will be a good match for you or vice versa, opportunities will present themselves much more often. Like we said earlier, your options and opportunities with women -- as well as your general state of well-being – will increase.

This book teaches men to be comfortable being our true selves, to be in the moment and to erase preconceived notions about women. We never aggressively push for women to like us nor do we talk ourselves up. Instead, we lead by following and focus more on listening so that we understand the women we are dating. We are in tune to the multifaceted nature of female behavior; their right to make their own decisions; and their subconscious and conscious avoidance of men who try to control them. We also learn the impressions that our own communications have on women.

When you learn this framework, you are learning a more or less predictable system that helps you alleviate much of the unpredictability of dating. When this unpredictability is reduced, you will feel more relaxed with women. For best results, you must practice and apply the system in your real-life interactions with women and have reinforcement training in order to assimilate it. Learning curves vary with each individual. Eventually, the system becomes absorbed into your personality and you don't have to think about it anymore. It becomes a part of you.

In a world filled with adversarial relationships in which the woman's system is stronger and more intuitive, how do we as men neutralize the imbalance while simultaneously setting ourselves up for success? Practice and learn the following concepts and have fun greatly increasing your success with women.

4

Concept 1: Attitude and Mindset
Do Women Really Like Bad Men?

For good reason, many men are internally conflicted on how to behave around the women we are attracted to. The reason this uncertainty exists is because women are generally also conflicted about the way they want or need men to behave around them. Women know intuitively when a man is behaving in an attractive manner but a majority of women cannot seem to verbalize exactly what "it" is that the man is doing that is attractive to her.

Have you ever heard a woman complain, "Why am I only attracted to bad guys and jerks?" I bet you have heard that one before. It's usually followed up with something like, "I just want a nice guy BUT I am just not attracted to nice guys." You may have noticed that women usually make this statement with a wry smile on their faces, because even they sense it's a puzzling, ironic and bizarre thing to say. How are we men supposed to take that? Are we supposed to mistreat a woman in order to win her over? That doesn't seem to make sense.

Women's perceived attraction to bad guys is so prevalent that it deserves some careful attention. Let me now ask you some questions that you may have been asking yourself for years. What does being a bad guy or a jerk mean exactly and why do women think that they are attracted to this type of man? How precisely does one purposely act like a bad guy or jerk to achieve results with women? And is being "bad" really a bad thing?

Ken had been dating Sharon for about a week when he began implementing the advice of his friend Scott, who told him, "If you want this thing to work, remember women love jerks." Since he really liked Sharon, Ken began acting accordingly. He didn't want to make the same mistakes he had with his past relationships, which he believed failed because he was too nice a guy – and thus came off as desperate. Ken's behavior led him to do the following: he didn't call Sharon when he said he was going to, he stood her up on several occasions, he belittled her in front of his friends and family and put her down regularly. Ken felt very conflicted acting this way to Sharon. He would juggle acting like his normal self and acting like a jerk, just to make sure he was "acting right" and not being too soft. Eventually, Sharon got sick and tired of his behavior and rightly broke the relationship off. Frustrated with himself and the loss of someone he truly cared for, Ken couldn't figure out which part of his behavior Sharon was attracted to and what she didn't care for. Did Sharon leave Ken for being a jerk? Or was it that she found herself not attracted to him when he acted too nicely to her?

Some men never bother to ask themselves these questions. For those who do, the misinterpretations and erroneous guesses about their answers are often the root cause of inappropriate behavior and mistreatment that destroy men's relationships with women they want to be with. Throughout this chapter, we will get to the bottom of these questions and answer them in effort to help you behave more appropriately, in a way that will elicit attraction while also treating women with respect.

The Key: Healthy Indifference

You might be interested to know that a woman's attraction to bad guys and jerks is a slip-up of words, her own misinterpretation of what she really desires. It's because many women lack the vocabulary and awareness to express exactly what it is they do need and want. They don't want a jerk. They want someone who is not desperate. What women actually need and want are men who portray a certain attitude – an attitude of indifference, which is a facet of confidence.

Actually, one of the most misunderstood, nicest and honest things you can do for yourself and the woman you are with is to become *selectively or healthfully indifferent* towards her interest in you.

Someone who is indifferent to the dating situation, someone who can "take it or leave it" as to whether it works out is very, very attractive to women. That's because he is the opposite of desperate – and desperate is the single most unattractive thing you can be to a woman.

Unfortunately, nice guys often act desperate (many times, because they are desperate). Meanwhile, who is acting indifferent? Jerks! They really don't care about a woman's well-being. They just don't care, period. Since this is the opposite of desperate, a woman finds this behavior attractive. However, a relationship with this kind of guy ends badly for a woman because he is a jerk. What women want is a man who isn't desperate but who is a good guy.

This is the key. Being healthfully indifferent while genuinely caring for a woman's well-being.

In order for me to explain why this is the case, we first need to talk about our attitude. It's generally accepted in our culture that when we are in a great mood or have an upbeat, positive or enthusiastic attitude, it is easier to interact with women. We feel like we are beaming positive energy and conversation tends to flow, which allows both parties to act more relaxed. We think that the more positive and enthusiastic we are, the more likely we are to achieve some sort of success with women. Unfortunately, this mindset sets men up for potential disaster.

The pressures of daily life make it impossible to be enthusiastic all the time. People who seem like they are *always* in a great mood are scary to us because we know it can't be for real. Think of the teacher's pet in your elementary school class. The brown-nose at my elementary school reminded me of Kathy Lee Gifford. She was always so overly enthusiastic to anything we did in school that even then our entire class knew her behavior was suspect. We knew intuitively that her never-ending enthusiasm was fraudulent.

Every human being, male or female, goes through times when he or she feels down. It's very normal at some point or another to feel depressed. In fact, it's difficult to be super-positive when your life is not going as smoothly as you would like. *And if there is one thing you can always count on, it's that life will be uneven and difficult.*

Many men incorrectly believe they will succeed with women only if they appear to have a never-ending enthusiasm and upbeat attitude. Since this is so hard to do, many men turn to alcohol or drugs to quell inhibitions and help them feel enthusiastic and positive when interacting with women. They do this to avoid the down-in-the-dumps feelings, which they believe will be harmful in these interactions.

But get this: it's dangerous to rely on interacting with women when you are too up or in an overly enthusiastic mood. When you act overly enthusiastic, you run the risk of being perceived as fraudulent. It also looks desperate – like you're trying too hard – and that's the one thing you must avoid.

Desperation is never, ever attractive – and women can sense it a mile away.

You need to do something entirely new. You need to be indifferent, not desperate. When you start each interaction with a properly directed, indifferent attitude, both you and the woman will benefit. This attitude is much more balanced then being up or down. It allows you the ability to relax and be yourself.

There are two primary ways men can be indifferent to women. One is healthy and sensible while the other is unhealthy and harmful (a jerk).

1. Healthy Indifference - Indifference towards her interest in you including: indifference about her decision to go out with you, indifference regarding her becoming intimate with you, indifference regarding her involving herself in a relationship with you. You enjoy meeting a woman, you enjoy talking to her, but you are certainly not desperate. If something happens, fine. If not, fine.

After their third date, Max and Jessica began kissing goodnight in Max's car as soon as they arrived at Jessica's apartment building. After a while Jessica said, " I would invite you up, but I just want to take it slowly with you. I am so attracted to you." Max really cared about Jessica and thought to himself, "It's going to happen anyway, just invite me up already!!!" Max was well-versed, though, about healthy indifference. Instead of pressuring Jessica, Max said, "I sure want to come up now" -- telling the truth -- "but only when you're ready" -- indifferent to her decision. Max knew that as much as he wanted to go upstairs, Jessica needed to discover for herself that the time was right for her to invite him up. By Max showing patience, honesty and healthy indifference to

Jessica, he will get invited upstairs, it's only a matter of time. And when they are intimate, it will be a better experience because Jessica most likely will not be defensive because she has been given the space to make her own decision.

2. Unhealthy Indifference - Indifference towards her needs and her autonomy including: not complementing and nurturing her, indifference about her safety, indifference regarding her general well-being, indifference about the welfare of those close to her.

After their third date, Max and Jessica began kissing goodnight in Max's car as soon as they arrived at Jessica's apartment building. After a while Jessica said, " I would invite you up but I just want to take it slowly with you. I am so attracted to you." Max really did not care about Jessica and thought to himself, "It's going to happen anyway, just invite me up already!!!" So he said, "Listen, I have taken you for three dinners, and you keep pulling this shit every time we get back to your place. Come on, let's go upstairs." Feeling pressured, Jessica begins feeling very uncomfortable. She senses Max's impending anger and resentment. Max says again, "Come on, let's go upstairs," to which an uncomfortable Jessica replies, "I just think that's not a good idea yet." Max says sarcastically, "Great, get out of the car. I can't believe this is happening again. If I knew you were going to pull this over and over, I would have gone out with the guys tonight." Max drives away.

A harmful man possesses the unhealthy indifference of example two. Women can become attracted to these men because they can't tell the difference between healthy and unhealthy indifference.

There are so few men who exhibit healthy indifference that the only thing left is the unhealthy kind. This is precisely where the myth of women liking jerks and bad guys comes from. Why do women always ask why there are no good guys out there? The reason is that it is rare to find a man who possesses only healthy indifference: a respect for her autonomy and decision-making power along with the characteristic of direct honesty.

Many well-meaning men mistakenly interpret women's confusing statements about being attracted to bad guys. They come to believe that the sure route to a woman's heart is by treating her badly. Other well-meaning men pretend to completely ignore women to whom they are attracted because they think this behavior is attractive to women and perceived as "playing it cool." Both of these techniques initially begin with and display the harmful indifference in example two.

Fortunately, we now know that healthy indifference to her interest in you is the catalyst to her attraction. Can we now agree that the above techniques are not necessary and discard that inappropriate behavior?

So, when you are in the presence of a woman you find attractive, it is *perfectly all right* to:

- Compliment her if you really believe she is attractive; you don't have to ignore her.
- Walk up and talk to her; you don't have to pretend she is not there.
- Care about and acknowledge her and her needs; you don't have to treat her badly.

All you have to be is direct and honest about what you want in regard to the possibility of dating her. But you *remain indifferent* to:

- Her interest in you.
- Her decision to go out with you or not.
- Her decision to become intimate with you.

It is that kind of direct honesty, coupled with healthy indifference, that makes you attractive to a woman. It also causes you to act natural and balanced without having to be overly positive or "on" all the time. This laidback attitude of directness, honesty, treating her well by acknowledging her needs, and healthy indifference to her interest in you is perceived as concern for her needs. And she correctly perceives you as someone who is confident and trustworthy. If you'll notice, many of the screen actors we mentioned in the first chapter embody this laidback and relaxed attitude of frank honesty and healthy indifference.

When you adopt this attitude, an undercurrent begins to appear in your interactions with a woman that gently suggests that you do not *need* to be with her. You are not desperate. Instead, you *want* to be with her. But if it doesn't work out, fine. This is the mark of confidence. Both women and men understand the difference between "need" and "want," whether or not they've ever consciously thought about it. "Need" is perceived as unattractive; "want" is an attractive quality. "Wanting" a woman, without "needing" her, is a very important shift that will have great benefits to you.

Women's receptors are very sensitive to the perception of neediness, which is the opposite of confidence. Sometimes, when you care deeply about a woman's interest in you or her decision whether to become intimate with you, it is perceived as neediness. And this is a very unattractive quality. Women would much rather date a man who is confident and doesn't need to be going out with her but wants to be. While it is always a good idea to care deeply about the woman you are with and her needs, I urge you to become "indifferent" by giving up any control you think you may have over her decisions. *You can't control women or the outcome of their decisions. You can only control yourself. It's that letting go of her decision-making that actually makes you attractive to her!*

A solid and healthy "indifference" mindset gives men the freedom, authority and *willingness to walk away* from an interaction or relationship if need be. That means the ability to walk away if doing so is excruciatingly painful. It stems from a strong fundamental belief that *everything is meant to be.*

I would now like to share a story to help demonstrate why an indifferent attitude to a woman's interest in you and her subsequent decisions about dating you are so vital to our success.

Have you ever purchased a car? Many people dread the experience of buying a car at a dealership for precisely the same reason that many women become defensive around men. It's because they don't want to be pressured into doing something that's not right for them. How do you feel when a salesman is pressuring you into purchasing a major investment like a car? Both men and women avoid being pressured into taking action that we are not ready for.

Car Salesmen

Two salesmen arrived at the car dealership showroom for another day of selling cars. One was the top-selling salesman at the dealership, while the other was in last place. The top-selling salesman, as you might imagine, knew exactly how to interact with customers in order to make the most sales. He understood his customers' needs and he respected their buying habits. He focused on making sure that the customer got what she needed and felt good about it, even if that meant sending the customer to another dealership to purchase a different model car!

The top salesman cared deeply about his customers' needs and desires. However, he was indifferent to their decisions on whether to buy one of his cars. He wanted them to get what they needed, even if he didn't have it. This attitude – which took pressure off the customers and let them feel relaxed around him -- provided him with many repeat customers. It also granted him the freedom to walk away from a customer that was not a good match for what he had to offer or who was going to waste his time. He was a master at spending his time wisely with customers whom he felt would buy as well as pleasantly parting ways with customers that he felt would not buy from him or who would be better off driving a car sold by someone else. As a result of his attitude, he always ended the year with the most sales and a healthy commission check.

The last-place salesman had the opposite tack. He approached all potential clients with the attitude that he desperately wanted to close a sale with them, no matter whether he had a car they needed or not. His behavior made customers feel pressured. To get away from this uncomfortable pressure, they usually told him they would think it over -- which is a euphemism for saying no. Understandably, he never heard from these potential customers again.

The last-place salesman was unwilling and unable to walk away from any deal – even those that weren't right for his customers. He placed enormous pressure on himself to figure out a way to convince every customer to buy. As a result, he was unhappy – and he sold very few cars.

As you would expect, the top-selling salesman always looked forward to coming into work but the last-place salesman couldn't stand getting up in the morning for another day with no sales. After closing yet another deal, the top selling salesman began to talk with the last- place salesman.

"You look pretty down," said the top salesman.

"I feel miserable and exhausted," responded the last-place salesman. "I can't sell anything and I don't know why. Either these customers just don't like me or they are just plain idiots. Even when they are really interested in the car, either I don't play the situation right or they are just messing with me. I haven't gotten a commission check in months!"

"Maybe you're doing more work and putting more pressure on yourself than you have to," the other replied. "Let's figure out how to help you make some sales. Let me ask you a question. Tell me what the customer does or says that prompts you to step in to close a deal."

"They seem to show some interest in a car and make a comment, like they think the color or steering wheel is nice," said the last-place salesman.

"Then what happens?"

"I tell them I am eager to help them and they should come into my office. I start getting excited about the possibility of making the commission. I tell them all I need is some information, and I can have them driving the car off the lot today. Then, most of the time, they say that they're not ready. And when I tell them that I could give them a great deal if they buy today, it ends up with them politely saying, 'I'll think it over.' And then they leave, never to return."

The top salesman thought for a minute about this and then asked, "When you get the sense that the customer seems interested in the car because they make the comment that they really like a particular feature, do you have any idea what's really happening in their mind?"

"Yeah, I can feel my commission check growing," said the last- place salesman.

"Not so fast," the other said. "What is actually going on is that the customer is in the beginning stages of buying a car. But she hasn't decided to buy it yet. She may want to get out and kick the tires, look at some other models or ask you more questions about it. If you put pressure on her to buy before she is ready, YOU come off like you really need the sale – not her. And all you get is an undecided potential client who feels uncomfortable that you are pressuring her. Remember, we are car salesmen. Unfortunately, there is a negative stigma that we are sneaky and devious so customers start out mistrusting our intentions. You've got to get the trust of the client by understanding her needs before you can make a sale. The potential client needs to feel you understand her – and she needs to be ready to buy – or else you are going to scare her away."

"So when she says she likes a car or something about it, she is not ready to be closed yet?" asked the last-place salesperson.

"Not yet. Here is what you do. When you sense that your customer is interested, that's good. But you need to be cautious. You're moving in the right direction but the sale is not complete yet. You want to become *indifferent* to her decision to buy the car. Then you want to pull her interest in the opposite direction."

"Why would I want to do that?"

"Because when you go in the opposite direction of her interest, you show t*hat you are more concerned with her buying the right car – the one that best suits her needs -- rather than your own need for a commission from the sale.* With this strategy, you focus on the customer's needs instead of your own needs. This attitude causes her to begin dropping her ingrained negative stigma of you as a car salesman. Once she begins to drop her wariness, she can relax and actually think about buying. In fact, she'll actually begin selling you on the reasons why she needs the car, while you sit back and relax."

"I kind of understand that," said the last-place salesman.

"I will share the secret of why I sell so much," said first-place salesman. "Think of it this way. Imagine every customer is a close friend of yours, and you only want what's best for her even if it means her leaving you and going to another dealership. You want what's best for her infinitely more then you want your commission check. Sometimes customers need something we can't give them. Although most salesmen cannot deal with that fact and fight against it, we can agree that for us guys in the know it's an acceptable scenario. If you approach your customer this way, you will treat her differently because you won't interfere with her power to make her own decisions to get what she needs. The customer intuitively realizes that you are different from the other salesmen because you have her best interests at heart. You are indifferent to her decision. If she buys from you, fine. If not, fine. Whatever is best for her. When you have this attitude, it allows her the freedom to make her own decisions without being pressured. And she'll want to do business with you because she realizes that you are indifferent to her decisions, which means you really do respect her and care about her. You really do want her to make the decision that's best for her. It's intuitive, understand?"

Although this approach felt very foreign to the last-place salesman, he hesitantly agreed to give it a try. He treated the next customer like a dear old friend, for whom he wanted only the best. In his mind, he decided to approach this sale as if he didn't need the commission, especially not from this "dear old friend." He acted as though he wanted only what was best for her. *He put the money out of his mind.* When this customer said she really "liked that red sporty car," he used his new attitude to do the opposite of what he normally would do in that situation. Instead of pressuring the customer to sign the deal in his office right away so he could get his commission, he patiently listened to her and then went in the opposite direction of what she said, in order to make sure she was getting what she needed and felt good about it.

He said, "That's a good car, of course. But I am concerned because it is a two-seater, and it seemed from our earlier conversation that you might need more room than that."

The woman responded, "Well I really do like it, and it's got enough room for my stuff. And it has all the options that I need."

As if he were dealing with an old dear friend – someone he wanted to make sure did the right thing for herself -- the last-place salesman said, "I want to make certain it has all the features you said you wanted so that it's a good match for you. If it doesn't, we can keep looking. Can you go over the features you said you wanted again, so we can make certain this car is a good match?"

She responded, "I like the gas mileage because of my long drive to work, the color red is my favorite, the financing package fits in my budget, etc...."

At this point, the customer was actually selling the last-place salesman on why the car was a good match for her. So when the last place salesman said, "Are you sure? It's everything you need, but I am still concerned about the space issue," the woman replied, "The space thing doesn't worry me. I really like this car. I'll take it." In other words, she closed the deal herself. And, a few minutes later, she became his first of many satisfied clients.

As you might have imagined, the car sales example is analogous to dating. The initial behavior of the last-place salesperson is the way most men act when approaching women. Unaware of the best approach – and unwilling to have the patience to overcome the initial suspicions women have about our intentions -- we push harder. Like annoying car salesmen, we do or say anything to pressure women to become intimate or commit to a relationship before they are ready. When we are dating and women show even a slight bit of interest in us, we often become super-pushy and aggressive. This is the worst thing we can do. It reveals our underlying neediness – which is not an attractive quality -- and it results in women feeling pressured. And then we wonder what we did wrong and why a woman is not returning our phone calls......

Like it or not, when you meet a new woman, you are as suspect to her as a car salesman. She suspects that your intentions are not based on what she wants or needs but solely on what you want. It is very difficult to convince a woman that she should want to be with a man she does not already desire let alone a man she hardly knows. So the more you try to convince her though pressure, the more she will become defensive. You're like a bad car salesman. Remember – women are looking for intimacy and relationships too. They just don't want to be pressured into them. Like the top salesman advised, we must learn how to lead women to discover for themselves that a decision to be with you can be advantageous for them.

We must learn how to lead women to close the deal themselves. We do this by using a technique called "Staying Onsides."

Staying Onsides

Staying Onsides is a technique that men who are intuitive with women naturally use. *Instead of moving towards a woman's interest in him, the man gently moves away from it, thereby causing the woman to "sell herself" to you.*

Staying Onsides is, at the most basic level, a system of giving and taking away while interacting with women. Either you or the woman you are with gives interest -- and then you it take away. If you do it long enough, attraction starts building. But there is a limit as to how much taking away you can do.

Have you have ever gone to a store to purchase a certain product only to get there and find that the store was sold out of the product? How did that make you feel? Did you want it more? You had interest in purchasing the product. Now that it's sold out, you want it even more.

This technique in the dating situation reverses the unwritten rule that says men must be enthusiastic and in charge of "selling" themselves to women. Staying Onsides says that approach is wrong. Instead, we allow women to make their own decisions. And men can relax and be comfortable with our true selves.

In football, what happens if the defensive team crosses the line of scrimmage before the center snaps the ball and the play begins? Off- sides penalty. In soccer, what happens if an offensive player runs onto the other team's half of the field ahead of the last defender without the ball? Off-sides penalty. When dating women, what happens if a man gets ahead of a woman's interest in him? You guessed it -- Off-sides penalty!

Let's turn to the Scale of Female Interest in men to find out what happens exactly.

Scale of Female Interest

-Negative- 0-1-2-3-4-5-6-7-8-9-10 *+Positive+*

When you meet a woman, her interest towards you can be measured one of three ways: Some version of enthusiastic (positive), unenthusiastic (negative) or indifferent (neutral).

Let's say that a woman at ten (10) is very enthusiastic and interested in having some kind of relationship with you, a woman at zero (0) is unenthusiastic and uninterested in having a relationship with you, and a woman at five (5) is indifferent to you; that is, she is neither interested nor uninterested in having a relationship with you.

Here is a scenario: You are on a date or at party with a woman who is at five (5). She doesn't seem to care about you one way or the other. At six

(6), she is more interested in you, as she passes seven (7), eight (8), and nine (9), she becomes more and more interested. If you can get this woman to move all the way up the scale to ten (10) she will want to go out with you again, become intimate and/or commit to a relationship.

By the same token, this woman can move down the scale. At four (4), she has less interest in ever seeing you again, as she passes by three (3) and two (2), she might start getting really unpleasant and upset, and at (1), she might even want to end the conversation with you right then and there. If she gets to zero (0), she will get up and leave.

Every woman's interest in you can be measured on this simple scale. And all women react rather predictably against the scale. When women are moving in either an enthusiastic or unenthusiastic direction on the scale, they are moving forwards (towards ten (10)) or backwards (towards zero (0)) on the scale, regardless of which point they are currently located -- with the exception of an inactive five (5). When women are inactive on the scale, they continue to be inactive. They stay at rest. This leads us to a very important rule of female behavior inspired by Newton's first law of motion – sometimes referred to as the "law of inertia."

A woman at rest tends to stay at rest and a woman in motion tends to stay in motion.

It doesn't matter if a woman is enthusiastic or unenthusiastic towards you; as long as she has some type of positive or negative interest, then she is moving. And when a woman is moving, it's only a matter of time before she becomes enthusiastic – when you Stay Onsides, that is, behind her interest in you. Women who are indifferent towards you are inactive. So we have to get them moving. We do this by Staying Onsides and jolting them by being more unenthusiastic than they are about their interest in you.

Combining this rule of female behavior with Staying Onsides gives men a gigantic boost when interacting with women!

Let's say you're out to dinner and you determine the woman you're with is at about seven (7) on the scale. Then she says, "I really like you, Bob." Many men will take this compliment and start acting really excited, giddy and enthusiastic. They believe the women is now at a ten (10) on the scale and they believe that their sexual and personal needs are all locked up. They might say something like, "Well, let's go back to my apartment and have some drinks and get to know each other even better."

Big mistake.

Although she likes you, the woman at seven (7) on the scale is not totally convinced and enthusiastic that you are a good match for her. She will not feel that way until she arrives at ten (10). But a woman who senses that a man is acting too enthusiastic or too emotional before she has made her decision will start moving in the opposite direction, towards unenthusiastic. For example, let's say she is at seven (7) when you say, "Well, let's go back to my apartment and have some drinks and get to know each other even better." This sends her down to a six (6) – or lower. And she responds with something like, "I am not sure that's a good idea so soon." You are suddenly caught off-sides and both of you feel uncomfortable.

Women act like this because in the early stages of an interaction with a man, there has not been enough trust established yet for her to feel safe about moving further ahead. And many men don't have the patience it takes to establish this trust. Like we mentioned earlier, women fear that they will end up being pressured into making a decision that may not be right for them. When men act too enthusiastic towards a woman's interest it leads women to become unenthusiastic in order to protect themselves. They run the other way on the scale. What do most men do when women run the other way and become unenthusiastic? They believe they should show more enthusiasm. They become very emotional and basically beg her.

You might say something like, " Come on, we will have a great time!" or "Don't be like that!" Or "Just come over and have some fun!" or "Trust me, I only want what's best for you." These statements are examples of needy and aggressive behavior that will only create distance between you and your date.

It's true that on some rare occasions a woman will respond to these statements by becoming intimate with you. But that often leads to other problems in the future (like withdrawing later). Most likely, when women witness this pushy behavior by men, they become wary again. They sense a man's neediness, which is the opposite of confidence – and which is a big turn-off.

Let's take the same situation -- a woman at seven (7) on the scale -- and demonstrate how you can, by Staying Onsides, influence the interaction more favorably. When the woman at seven (7) on the scale says, "I really like you, Bob," you would be sensible to respond by simply saying, "Thank you for the compliment. Well, since we don't know each other that well yet, there is a lot more to me that you will have to decide if you like or not."

You are Staying Onsides and behind her interest – you have displayed yourself as at a six (6) or so on the scale, which is behind her seven (7). This non-emotional response didn't put any negative pressure on your date by getting ahead of her interest in you – which we know is Off-sides in No Man's Land. You did not get crazy-excited with the compliment.

Instead, you remained calm and used your Staying Onsides acumen.

The woman might then respond with, "You're right, I don't know you that well. But you seem nice enough -- or maybe you could just be putting on a good show." This shows she's moved down to a five (5) or a four (4). You could respond with something like, "Maybe there is something you could ask me to find out if I am really genuine. You could ask me about my family or..."

Let's say the woman is now down to four (4) on the scale but begins asking you more questions about yourself. You might be thinking the woman's interest is actually going in the opposite direction of ten (10), which is where we want her to be. Remember, woman that are moving on the scale are always in motion, whether they're going up or down the scale. And as long as men stay at least one number behind a woman's interest, women that are moving will eventually become enthusiastic if valid *aching* (motivational factors) is present.

Think of it this way: *Never become more enthusiastic than the woman you are with.* Never get ahead of her interest in you. When she is at eight (8), you move to seven (7). When she is at four (4), find safer ground at three (3). When you get in front of a woman's interest, it's like putting the cart before the horse. Off-sides penalty! Women become scared when this happens and -- depending on how much trust has been previously established -- may choose not to be with you. If you get in the way of your own happiness, you have nobody to blame except yourself. When you continue to patiently Stay Onsides, you end up leading women to ten (10).

Imagine now that you are at a party with a few of your buddies and you strike up a conversation with a small group of women. One woman in particular seems really attractive and intriguing to you and you would certainly like to get to know her better. Your

43

attempts at talking with her are failing. She is answering you with one-word responses, isn't smiling and you determine she is at five (5) or indifferent to you.

I have witnessed many men in this very situation. They usually will mishandle it one of two ways. First, many men will turn up the enthusiasm and basically act like they're at a ten (10) on the scale. They show even more excitement towards the woman and say things that are really positive in hopes it will have a rewarding effect on the woman. This type of behavior is conducive to finding yourself off-sides. It will only make her more guarded. Second, many men may resort to saying something like, "Why aren't you smiling?" which will certainly make her feel uncomfortable. Again, this type of behavior will only make her more guarded.

An intuitive man would realize that the women is indifferent at five (5) and that he needs to get her in motion. He realizes that becoming enthusiastic or super-positive would mean getting ahead of her interest in him. Instead of going off-sides, he will move even lower on the scale than the woman, let's say, to a three (3). This position is a much safer place for the man to be. He might say something like, "I think you're really attractive, but you're probably closed-minded to meeting new men, right?" That's an example of an unenthusiastic Onsides jolt to get her moving. It's like jumping life into a dead car battery. Staying Onsides by moving in a way that's even less enthusiastic than the woman may cause her to become more or less enthusiastic towards you. But that doesn't matter. *What matters is that she starts moving in either direction!*

Even if she becomes unenthusiastic and responds with a comment like, "I am not closed-minded! Who do you think you are?" she is now moving. And as we learned before, women that are moving stay in motion. And women in motion will

44

eventually move in a positive direction, if enough *aching* (motivational factors) is present in her life. An intuitive man would continue to become more unenthusiastic and say something back like, "I guess it doesn't make sense to talk. I can walk away, if that's what you want." At this point, the woman has nowhere to go but to become more enthusiastic or risk ending the interaction all together. Most of the time, the woman will become more positive – as long as you stay comfortably behind her interest. And if she wants you to walk away, it's most likely because she doesn't have the *necessary aching (motivational factors)* and the two of you *were not meant to be.*

Let's take a quick look at how this attitude and mindset satisfy some of the previously confusing questions we may have had in the past.

Q: Why does it seem so difficult to meet women when you are single but when you already have a girlfriend or are married, the opportunities seem more plentiful?

A: Men who are dating or married tend to naturally display only healthy indifference toward women because their commitments require them to be indifferent to other women's interest in them. Because they are indifferent, they automatically are more attractive to other women.

Q: Why is it the case that when you are dating a woman and lose interest in her, she ends up being extremely attracted to or interested in you?

A: Men that are dating women they are generally uninterested in will automatically display some form of healthy indifference. Again, this is attractive to the woman.

Q: Why is it that when you terminate relationships with women that you are not interested in, you sometimes become attracted to them again when they start dating someone else?

A: Women that were once overly needy can easily become healthily indifferent to you when they find a new love interest. When they are indifferent to you, they become more attractive than when they were needy.

Q: Why are attractive women who act in a negative way towards men very intimidating and hard to approach?

A: These attractive and negative women usually start off very unenthusiastic on the scale near two (2) or three (3). Many behave this way as a defense mechanism. Unfortunately, since many men start at an enthusiastic ten (10), we often find ourselves off-sides and completely unable to illicit interest in these women. As long as men Stay Onsides and start off a little more unenthusiastic than these women, they most likely will become more pleasant to be around – and more receptive.

Q: Why are men attracted to "teases?"

A: It is easy for most men to be taken by a tease. Women who are teases start off very enthusiastic on the scale, near eight (8) or nine (9). Unlike attractive but negative women, they are pleasant to be around at the onset of an interaction. Therefore, many men feel safe starting off–sides at ten (10). However, these women use their enthusiasm or pleasantness as a defense mechanism. They will continually slide down the scale unless men know to Stay Onsides.

Since you can never control a woman's decision-making process – that is, her decision about whether to date you -- I suggest you *let go* and become indifferent to her interest in you. And when we let go, women sense it. They realize what a wonderful man you are because you respect their autonomy. The fact that you are indifferent – which means confident and the opposite of needy – makes you more attractive. It's like a boomerang of good energy. You let go of trying to control the woman and your good will comes back to you tenfold. Displaying healthy indifference to her decision to be with you is actually a very caring way for us to be. Instead of our feelings being up or down depending on a woman's decision – one that we can't control in the first place – we allow them their natural right to have the power over their decisions. And we respect their decisions, whatever the result. Women are always attempting to make the best decision possible for themselves – and we should respect that.

Through this healthy indifference to another person's actions we are not buffeted around by things we can't control. We are in balance. We no longer "need" to be with a particular woman -- we "want" to. We are the opposite of needy. We are confident. Over time, as you venture further into a meaningful relationship, your healthy indifference begins to blossom into an ever-growing respect for her autonomy.

5

Concept 2: Trust Building Toolkit
Opposites Do Not Attract; They Get Divorced

You're about to go on a date with a woman that you find very attractive. What are you thinking? Is it something like, "I hope she is attracted to me so we can be intimate!"

Let me pose a question to you. What if you could know, in advance, that at a minimum she (or any woman you are dating, for that matter) would perceive that the two of you hit it off every time? You would know the two of you would get along even before you spent time with her. Your mindset would change, wouldn't it? It would go from hoping she likes you, to you deciding whether or not *you* like *her* – and whether she is a good match for you .

In this chapter, we are going to explore the tools that will allow you to strengthen your attitude and build trust with a woman. There are certain techniques that have been developed through the study of Transactional Analysis (TA) and Neuro-Linguistic Programming (NLP). If practiced correctly, they can pretty much ensure that you will click with a vast majority of the women you are with. Through your verbal and non-verbal behavior, you will be able influence a women both subconsciously and consciously to feel comfortable with you.

Eric Berne, a psychiatrist in San Francisco, developed the beginnings of what was to become TA in the late 1950's. Berne studied how people dealt or interacted with one another and how people could enrich their lives by altering their behavioral mistakes. This was a revolutionary idea because most psychiatrists at the time focused on what went on inside of people instead of *between* them. Berne pioneered many ideas used in the field of behavior modification.

While we will briefly touch on concepts from Berne's work throughout this book, it is important that we now extract some TA- inspired principles for the purpose of this chapter on trust-building. Here are a few ground rules inspired by TA.

1. Always make a woman you are with feel good and comfortable; in fact, make sure she feels even better than you feel yourself. This seems like common sense. But we mean having your mind or internal editor checking this rule against everything you do and say. It requires you to be totally in the moment – instead of thinking ahead to what's down the road with her. But do this without being phony – which will be perceived as desperate. And desperation, as we now know, is the death of success.

2. Flipping your ego inside out is a good way to begin each dating situation. Our ego's main job is to get our needs met. By flipping our ego inside out, we become more focused on understanding and meeting the needs of the woman we are with instead of our own needs. An adage that confident men follow is this: *When women get their needs met, they are more than happy to help men get their needs met.* So flipping our ego inside out and totally focusing on the woman's needs is really in our own best interest.

3. No Games. Since we are dropping the adversarial dynamic because it doesn't work that well for us, let's agree to be assertive, direct and honest instead of playing games. No lies. No phony compliments.

4. Avoid acting superior to women. This helps us avoid playing a game called one-upmanship, and it also gives you a greater chance of helping the woman get her needs met. Allow women you are with to know more than you know or to be smarter than you are.

5. You don't have to be Mr. Perfect. Self-deprecating humor is the most appropriate humor to employ while dating. In addition, it's perfectly okay to admit not knowing or understanding something -- or needing help -- when dating or interacting with women. In fact, it can be very disarming because it allows women to drop many of their preconceived notions about men. You are non-aggressive when you're not Mr. Perfect. This approach forces you to act assertive but relaxed instead.

6. Address major problems before they come up in order to build trust. Everyone has personal problems of some kind or another. If you have a recurring problem that interferes with your dating life, bring it up as soon as it's appropriate. This helps build trust, keeps you acting naturally and, if this person isn't going to be a good match, then you want to know sooner rather than later.

Jack picked Nancy up for their first date. He noticed that Nancy was noticeably very nervous. Since Jack also got nervous at the beginning of first dates, he expressed his own nervousness by telling Nancy, "I was so nervous before I picked you up that I circled around the block a couple times." Nancy was so surprised by Jack's comment that she said, "Really?" and actually repeated what he had told her back to him. In addition her entire posture changed, she smiled and began becoming more comfortable. By Jack's admission of severe nervousness, he allowed Nancy to be more comfortable than he was. He allowed her to become more comfortable by revealing his own discomfort.

Why would Jack do this? Because Jack knows that Nancy's comfort level with him is crucial for trust building. In addition, since Jack has flipped his ego inside out he is totally focused on Nancy getting her needs met (which means he can get his met).

Since Jack was being honest and was not playing games he set a strong opening "no" agreement which you will learn about in chapter six. This caused Nancy to feel even more comfortable around Jack, even though she didn't realize exactly why it made her feel comfortable at the time.

Later in the evening, Nancy began explaining her love of travel to Jack. She told him about how she had taken a dream vacation to Italy and all the sights she had seen. Jack, who had been to Italy five times and toured extensively, allowed Nancy to explain each site and what she liked about it and why. He avoided acting what could be construed as superior by refraining from trumping her travels with his much more extensive exploration of Italy. He allowed her to share her happy memories.

As the two headed back to Jack's car, Jack actually walked in the wrong direction by *accident, and Nancy pointed it out to him. Embarrassed, Jack began making fun of his questionable sense of direction. He said," I could get lost in my own driveway if I wasn't careful." Jack knows that nobody is perfect and he didn't have to be Mr. Perfect for Nancy to be attracted to him.*

Nancy then suggested to Jack that the two go for cocktails before he dropped her off. Jack took a deep breath and said that he couldn't do that and there was something he wanted to share with Nancy. He said, "Unfortunately, I can't do that tonight or any night for that matter. I want you to know that I am an alcoholic and I have not had a drink in over two years. I have had problems in the past with my behavior when I drink. Does that bother you?" Nancy, without missing a step, said that it didn't bother her and the two went for coffee instead upon her suggestion. Jack was happy that his admission didn't seem to really faze Nancy. Jack was also confident enough to realize that if his admission of being an alcoholic did really trouble Nancy that she wouldn't be a good match for him.

When you begin to employ these basic steps, you will be in the beginning stages of laying a solid foundation of building trust on a conscious level. Now, Neuro-Linguistic Programming (NLP) will help us to ensure women trust you on a subconscious level.

NLP was developed by John Grinder, a linguist, and Richard Bandler, who at the time was a computer programmer and mathematician. The two men spent time studying a variety of long-accepted concepts of psychology. They organized these concepts into a body of knowledge known as NLP for the purpose of studying the ongoing process of coding excellence. One of the pieces to NLP regarding interpersonal communication and human behavior makes good sense when you compare it to an earlier finding of Sigmund Freud. Freud established the idea that the subconscious mind was infinitely more powerful than the conscious mind. NLP organized a technique called "matching," which allows men to build trust directly with a woman's subconscious.

Body Language

According to NLP, more than half of the trust established between men and women comes from physiology, which means body language. If you have ever visited a social worker, psychologist, or psychiatrist, you may be surprised to learn that they most likely matched your body movements when you were in session with them. They copied how your body was positioned! The reason? It's an extraordinarily effective technique to help patients become comfortable with them and trust them. If clients don't trust their doctors, they will not share all the personal and often painful information the doctor needs to help them solve whatever problems they have.

I first began noticing this when a social worker that I was seeing in the late '90s almost kicked over a lamp in her office for about the fifth time while I was visiting her for a session. When I asked her if she was all right, she shared with me that she was trying to cross her left leg over her right, the same way I usually sit. This was not a naturally comfortable thing for her to do and, on top of that, there was a large and unsteady lamp very close to her right side.

In accordance with a rule of human dynamics, women feel most comfortable with men who are like them.

When you match a woman's body movements, a message starts to form subconsciously in her mind

53

that, "This guy is like me and I like that." You do not have to be concerned that women will think you are strange when you are matching them. Women are not conscious that the matching is taking place. It almost always happens on a subconscious basis.

When you are in the presence of a woman that you would like to feel comfortable with you, begin to match her body movements. If you are both sitting at a restaurant table, for example, and she has her left leg crossed over her right leg, do the same thing. If she has her arms folded, fold your arms too. Remember, as you become a reflection of her, she subconsciously begins to relax and feel more comfortable with you. You do not have to read into or try to interpret what her body language means. Just match it. It is also important to note if she has any nervous habits; for instance, playing with her hair or tapping a foot on the floor. Do not match that. Matching nervous habits comes off as obnoxious and will not make her feel comfortable and good about herself. Stick to her basic body physiology, such as her leg and arm positioning. If she is leaning backward or forward, if her head naturally tilts one way or the other, if her hands are clamped or if one elbow is resting on the table, do the same yourself. Reflect her eye contact and facial expressions and you will be fine.

Let me illustrate further to help you understand why this is important and how it naturally happens anyway. Think of a good friend or family member with whom you are close. What makes your relationship so comfortable, at a level that is not true for other acquaintances? Do you use the same slang words? Think the same things are funny? Next time you are together, pay attention to how he or she is positioned physically. Friends or family members who are close usually have the same posture. They move and gesture in similar ways, laugh together and adopt the same style, pace and rhythm in conversation and movement. Ever answer the phone in your house and someone told you, "I was certain you were your father or brother!" Good friends and family members often match and copy each other. This happens naturally when people are in rapport. We usually aren't consciously aware this is happening but nevertheless it almost always is. Once you're aware of this, you'll begin to notice it all around you.

If you have ever watched animals during play, they tend to match each other as well. When dogs play, they match each other by dropping down on their front two paws with their tails up in the air. It's hard-wired into humans and animals alike. We cannot help but like people who act like us.

The other benefit of matching is that it helps us pay careful attention to the women we are with. When you are matching women, you tend to become very in tune with what they are feeling, to the point that you may start getting strong gut feelings as to their state of mind at a deeper level then you ever imagined. I suggest you learn to trust these gut level feelings. Always trust your gut.

In the rare case that the woman you are with is so self- aware that she realizes you are matching her, feel free to tell her the truth – but only if she asks you. Tell her you have been matching her because it helps you pay close attention to her and you want her to feel comfortable with you. Most women appreciate being the center of your attention and feeling they are the only woman in the room.

Women's Tonality

Now that we know that women like men who are a reflection of them and that more than half of trust-building is established by body language, realize that it's also the case that women like men who sound like them. Your tonality -- the way you sound to women -- is important. According to NLP, tonality makes up close to forty percent of building trust.

Bradley Fenton

Have you ever noticed the actress Fran Drescher, who starred in "The Nanny" television series? While we can agree that she is a beautiful woman, the exaggerated nasal honking of her character's voice was so annoying and piercing that it almost negated her beauty. She became less attractive when she opened her mouth. Maybe on television it was cute but in a real-life situation, wouldn't it get on your nerves eventually? Imagine that voice instructing you to take out the garbage. Does it make you feel comfortable and good or uncomfortable and bad?

When you listen to a woman talk, zero in on her volume, rate of speech, tone and the types of words she likes to use. It doesn't seem like how you sound would really matter, but it does.

Have you ever received a telemarketing call, where the representative was flying through his script at the speed of light? He was talking so fast that you didn't have time to think. That kind of thing has the tendency to make us very uncomfortable. With that example in mind, imagine you're a very soft-spoken, quiet women who likes to speak slowly and choose her words carefully, and you're on a date with a man who is talking so loud and fast you don't have time to think. His voice is practically shocking you. How would you feel in that situation -- comfortable and good? Would you say, "Wow, this guy has a great, loud, booming voice!" Or might you say to yourself, "This guy is a fast- talking player. I'm not sure I can trust him."

Some women talk softly while others are loud. Some talk slowly while others are fast. We need to pay attention to how women are speaking and adjust our voices accordingly. Imagine if you were in a library belting out a story of what happened during work yesterday or at a party last night. Might you ruffle some feathers and get some people annoyed at you? Some quiet women live their lives as if the world were their own peaceful library. Others like to talk loud and fast. Whatever it may be, respect a woman's tonality and adjust yours accordingly.

While women have their preferred style of tonality, they also have favorite words they like to use. It is important to listen for words that your date likes to use and repeat them back to her in conversation. If your date, Sally, mentions for the third time that she likes houses that have 'character' and she likes people that have 'character' and her little cousin is such a 'character', start fitting the word 'character' into your sentences. Play her favorite words back to her like a tape recorder. This will help you build 'character' with her!

Remember, more than half of trust-building is body language and close to 40 percent is tonality. Tonality matters when building relationships and making women feel comfortable. Now you're ready for the last 10 percent of building trust. It has to do with coming to our senses.

Women's Sensory Filtration and Verbal Preferences

Imagine you are at a baseball game. There are 50,000 people packed into the stands, all having conversations. There is a ball game going on, planes flying overhead, the smell of freshly cut grass, the taste of popcorn and peanuts, the feel of the plastic seats underneath you, kids screaming, etc. Our brains function a lot like computers. If we didn't have our five senses of sight, sound, touch, taste and feel, it would be safe to say that there would be too much going on for us to process at one time. It would be sensory overload and, like a computer, we would need to shut down -- most likely by passing out. We wouldn't be able to make sense of a baseball game or anything else going on, for that matter. We all need our senses to help us filter out various experiences so our brains can handle the information.

Of course, women's brains are like computers, too. When women are in a dating situation, there is a lot going on, wherever the interaction might be taking place. In fact, so much is happening that if women did not have the use of their senses, it would be too much for them to process and they would also need to reboot.

Women turn to their senses to understand what is going on during a date and to make decisions that will affect your future with her. Decisions like: Does she like you? Does she want to become intimate with you? Is there a potential for a future with you? Most people have one sense that is stronger or more dominant than the others. The senses that usually dominate are visual (sight), kinesthetic (touch, taste, feel) or auditory (sound).

Visual women like to make decisions based on pictures and images.
Can she see the two of you together?

Kinesthetic women make decisions based on the way they feel about something.
Is the relationship stifling and does it have her in a stranglehold?

Auditory women need to hear something to make a decision.
Is he telling me what I need to hear from him?

The senses work together but one usually takes precedence. You need to establish, very early on, which sense dominates in the woman you are with. In order to do this, you need to listen for clues in what she says while she is talking to you.

Visual women will say things like: "I am trying to *picture* that in my *mind's eye*. It was hard for me to *focus* on what she was saying. I could *see* where they were going with that." Visual women need to be able to see that you're a good match for them. If you are with a visual woman, you need to speak visually. "What *looks* good on the menu?" is a good question to ask a visual woman.

Kinesthetic Women will say things like: "It *feels* a bit *choppy* to me. They were *smooth* as silk. That was a *rough* task to accomplish." Women who are kinesthetic want to feel that you are a good match for them. If you are with a kinesthetic woman you need to speak kinesthetically. "Do you *feel* how *smoothly* the conversation is going?" is a good question to ask a kinesthetic woman.

Auditory Women will say things like: "I *hear* you on that one. She *spoke* as clearly as a *whistle*. That has a nice *ring* to it." Auditory women need to hear you say important things to them that help determine if you are a good match. If you are with an auditory woman, you need to speak in reference to sound. "That *rings* true to me," is a good statement to make to a woman that is predominantly auditory.

Once you know which sense dominates in the woman you are with, it is like having a blueprint on how to establish trust with her by understanding how she experiences the world. By listening for key words and becoming part of her sensory world, you build trust in ways she may rarely have experienced.

Good relationships are built on trust. When you use the trust-building toolkit, you are creating a scenario in which women will like you. It's human nature. When you understand that you have the ability to build trust with new women, it is important to adopt a "good-match agenda." Be selfish and find the very best match for yourself. As we discussed at the beginning of the chapter, most men enter new situations with women with the mindset that, "I hope she is attracted to me and I hope we click so we can be intimate." That's the old adversarial agenda that you need to discard. That agenda has been setting you up for disappointment. When you utilize and strengthen your trust-building skills, your agenda will slowly begin to change toward finding a good match. Using our self-control, we can have an enormous influence on building trust and clicking with women.

6

*Concept 3: The Opening "No" Agreement
Make "No" an Okay Answer -- and Hear "Yes" More
Often*

There is sometimes a great deal of strength in stating the obvious. And in dating situations, doing so can actually alter the entire dynamic of the interaction to make it more balanced and therefore favorable for men. The Opening "No" Agreement is a powerful and honest tool that will help you in interactions with women. If done correctly, it has several benefits:

1. It sets an intuitive agenda.
2. It helps you get rid of your nervous feelings.
3. The healthy indifference displayed in this technique will make you more appealing to women because you will be correctly perceived as confident and a man who understands the difference between "need" and "want."
4. It creates equilibrium with the second and third part of the woman's system.
5. She will feel more comfortable with you because you are respecting her decision-making ability.
6. It will even help her feel good if she chooses not to be with you.

Before we go into the specifics of the Opening "No" Agreement, we need to talk about the perceived powerlessness many men feel while interacting with women. Most men find it extremely nerve-racking to muster up the courage to assertively approach women. Yet we all understand that these initial interactions are necessary and crucial because there can be no subsequent relationship or intimacy without them. So why do we feel powerless and get those nervous butterflies when the time comes for us to take action or "make our move?" It stems from the modern-day adversarial relationship. We want to win – or, more fittingly, we are playing not to lose.

Most professional athletes will tell you that they get butterflies before their games as well. They realize that they are skilled at what they do but they badly want to win. The problem for a professional athlete, excluding financial considerations tied to performance, is that victory can be likely but it always remains unknown until the contest is over. Likewise in a dating situation, the decisions that women make are always an unknown. Therefore it's difficult for the man precisely because men have a fear of the unknown – what the women will decide -- as well as the fear of the associated risk of potential rejection.

One of the main principles of Transactional Analysis is that both men and women need at least a small amount of social fulfillment. As human beings, we need at bare minimum a little taste of acceptance. Because the dating world is filled with rejection that's exactly why dating and interacting with women is so difficult for many men. An Opening "No" Agreement makes it more bearable if a woman decides you are not right for her. It also rewards you for taking the first risk involved in starting the interaction.

An Opening "No" Agreement is effective and, when done appropriately, it dissolves much of the pressure involved with dating. It involves men making it clear to women at the onset of an interaction or date, in straight-forward terms, that it is acceptable for that woman to tell him, "No, we are not a good match for each other," and to end the interaction, date or relationship at anytime.

At the beginning of the first date, it may sound something like this:

"Stacy, I really think you look beautiful tonight and I want to tell you something that I feel is very important to say. My hope is that we hit it off and want to see each other again. But I want you to know that if you get an intuitive feeling that we are not a good match for each other, for whatever reason, it's okay to tell me 'No' and to tell me that, in your mind, we are not right for each other. I want you to know that if you come to that conclusion, I may be a bit disappointed but there will certainly be no hard feelings on my part. Are you okay with that?"

On the phone prior to a date, it may sound something like this:

"Rebecca, I want you to know that I am attracted to you or I wouldn't have asked you out in the first place. With that said, I understand that since we are just beginning to get to know one another, you might decide at some point, for whatever reason, that I am not a good match for you. I hope that doesn't happen but realistically it could. If you ever feel like that, I want you to know that it's all right for you to tell me 'No.' And I may be a little disappointed but we can part ways amicably. Does that make sense to you?"

When you make an Opening "No" Agreement, you are setting the stage for a scenario in which you cannot fail. Either the woman you are with accepts your agreement and will tell you no if she decides the two of you are not a good match or you move on to a woman who will accept the agreement. If she agrees to tell you no, you have given her permission to do so beforehand so it is not nearly as painful for either of you.

Most men think of dating and interacting with women as a purely emotional experience. The Opening "No" Agreement says that's incorrect, to some degree. The agreement allows dating or interacting to become a little less emotional and a little more intellectual by setting a sensible boundary. While there is always going to be a degree of emotion involved, for best results we need to be mostly intellectual about dating until a solid commitment is made.

Let's think of the early stages of a relationship, the first date for instance, as an intellectual process like an important business transaction or interview. Let's use buying a car for example. Would you ever buy a car without first making an agreement about what is going to take place during the transaction? No way! You would sit down and negotiate with the seller on the price, title, payment options, pick-up date, etc. In other words, a good businessperson figures out what potential problems could occur at the beginning of a deal and confronts them at that point. This avoids problems down the road.

Why can't we do the same thing as good businesspeople do? Establishing an Opening "No" Agreement is direct. It shows honesty and assertiveness because you are establishing a rule to overcome a problem that plagues most dating situations and you're taking care of it right upfront.

As you recall, most men get stuck in the stage of interaction in which they feel deceived when the woman suddenly disappears or doesn't return phone calls. She obviously feels the two of you are not a good match but doesn't want to tell you. This behavior by women ends up causing much of the confusion, arguments and despair that happen during dating. The reason this happens is because many women are afraid to tell men that they are not attracted to us or that we are not a good match for them – and, the truth is, we are often too fragile to hear it. The excuses women make for their own inability to say no sound something like: "I didn't want to hurt his feelings" or "I wanted to let him down slowly." Know that although women usually say they don't want to hurt you (and this is probably true), they certainly are not doing men any kind of public service by behaving this way.

Some women fail to tell men no for their own selfish reasons. If a woman cannot say "No" without feeling bad or guilty about herself, then she will not do so. Some women find it easier to mislead you or disappear, hoping that you will "get the hint" eventually. This way, they never have to confront their own possible need for approval because they don't want you to say anything that might cause them to feel that they are bad people.

By communicating directly and in no uncertain terms that it is okay for women to tell us "No" we are making it very clear that it is not acceptable behavior for women to deceive us or to disappear if they don't feel like we are a good match for them. The Opening "No" Agreement places a gentle pressure on women if they choose to mislead us by not returning phone calls or by disappearing. It's a healthy, adult kind of pressure, which makes it more likely that women will treat us as the equals we are.

We choose to display courage when we first meet women by taking the action and the risk of asking them out in the first place. With the Opening "No" Agreement, women are more likely to take the risk of telling us directly, openly and honestly if they feel we are not a good match for them. If a woman lacks the courage and honesty to tell you "No" after you made it very clear that she has that option, she deserves to be uncomfortable and stuck in the relationship until she does. And if she disappears or misleads you, you have the right to be angry and disappointed with her. She is not being honest or forthright and you may at that point come to the realization that she is not a good match for you!

Broken down into its components, the Opening "No" Agreement simply addresses what is really happening during the interaction:

1. You are physically attracted to a woman and would like to spend time with her to determine whether or not the two of you are a good match.
2. At the end of the date, she will need to make a decision if she wants to see you again.
3. If she wants to see you again, that's great and you will go out again. If she does not, she has the right to say No, and you agree that No is an acceptable answer. You part ways amicably.

The Opening "No" Agreement is an assertive way to help improve your success with women. You are not guaranteed that every woman will want to spend time with you but at least you will know where you stand. And it will strengthen your instincts about when women are playing games. At first glance, it may seem like an easy agreement to say out loud but if you're having trouble getting the words out of your mouth in front of a woman, that's understandable. It takes a great deal of courage to make an Opening "No" Agreement because it will involve you confronting the reality of the situation, coming to terms with the possibility of you and your date not being a good match, and calls for you to change your behavior. It's normal if you fumble through your words the first few times in front of a woman. I urge you to practice making an Opening "No" Agreement at home and then apply it to your dating interactions. To hear the word "yes" more often -- and have more fun and less pressure dating than you ever thought was possible -- let's decide to make "No" an okay answer.

7

Concept 4: Questions and Aching
The Aching Truth About Asking Good Questions

Imagine you just got into a car accident out in the countryside. You didn't see some black ice and spun out, ramming your car into a ditch. After blacking out for a while, you come to and notice that your leg is badly hurt (a bone is actually protruding from your shin area) and you are having intense stomach pains. You are in desperate need of medical attention. You manage somehow to squeeze yourself out of the car and flag down a passing motorist, who agrees to take you to the nearest hospital.

When you arrive at the hospital, you are taken by wheelchair into a triage room to await an examination from the doctor on call. At this point your stomach feels like it is going to explode and you are very concerned. After a brief wait, the doctor finally walks in and introduces himself to you.

"Hello, my name is Dr. Herbson and that's a nasty-looking broken leg," he tells you. Then he continues talking. "I want you to know that I have a very wonderful practice going at this hospital. I attended Yale as an undergraduate and got my medical degree from Harvard. I am a specialist and pride myself in being one of the best internists in the state. Last year, I received numerous awards for my outstanding surgical skills. In fact, I am so recognized among my peers that I was just invited to speak at a medical conference in Switzerland. Not only are the organizers paying for my entire trip to Switzerland but they have also offered me $50,000 to talk about how to perform my specialty, which is leg surgery. With my skills as a surgeon, I should be a chief of surgery at a prominent city hospital in the near future. When that happens, I want to move my wife and daughters into a large mansion and then purchase a summer home and a boat because we love to be on the water. Which reminds me -- once, when I was fishing..." He continues for several minutes.

Furious and in pain, you interrupt his rant and ask him to please examine you. He tells you, "Your leg will be like new. Don't worry about a thing because I am so talented," and then continues talking. You're still wondering what is wrong with your stomach and the *aching* pain is increasing in intensity. He has never bothered to ask if anything other than your leg hurts and he continues to cut you off when you desperately try to point your stomach pain out to him. You feel helpless and misunderstood.

This extremely bizarre behavior, we hope, will never happen if you visit a physician. Good doctors are trained to patiently focus on your needs during an examination and not to jump to conclusions, make guesses based on exterior observations, make petty assumptions or to focus the examination on themselves. Your aches and pains need to be the focus of the interaction and thoroughly diagnosed and treated. Good doctors must ask questions and listen in order to meet the patient's needs.

Like good doctors, men must realize that a woman's needs must become the focus of our interactions. Every woman (like a medical patient) has needs when you interact with her and your job is to understand and acknowledge those needs. The cool thing is that we don't have to try and fix them. Understanding their needs is all that is needed in order for her to feel comfortable.

Unfortunately, many men can be awfully similar to Dr. Herbson when interacting with women. We talk too much and don't listen nearly enough. We are more focused on getting our own needs met rather than meeting the women's needs. The more you listen and understand the needs of the woman you are with, the more you will get your own needs met -- and the more successful with women you will become. So let's agree, like good doctors, that we should focus on the needs of the women we are with.

While growing up, many men mistakenly learned from society that the most productive way to succeed with women is to try to talk them into wanting to be with us. Instead, we should lead women to that point instead of telling them or trying to convince them to do so. Leading women -- instead of telling and convincing them -- has two benefits. First, if you remember back to the car salesman example, a decision that a woman makes for herself is much more powerful than one she makes after being pressured into something she may not be ready for. Women must be allowed to make their own decisions – and we have to respect those decisions.

Second, when we are trying to tell or convince a woman, we end up talking the majority of the time instead of listening. If we want to succeed with women, it needs to be the other way around.

The reason for much of our trouble is that many men have difficulty getting women to do most of the talking. This problem stems from the fact that most men dislike silence, detest normal pauses in communication and don't ask enough questions. We end up filling silence by talking and spouting out gibberish or verbalizing just about anything that comes to mind. It is partly this mindless gibberish that ends up getting us into trouble. When we speak without putting any thought into our words, how can we determine if what we are saying is making the woman we are with feel comfortable?

Silence

You might be surprised to know that silence and normal pauses during dating situations and interactions with women can actually be a wonderful thing instead of something to be feared. If used correctly, silence is another powerful tool to help create equilibrium between men and women. Silence in certain situations actually shows respect to women because their needs become our focus and warrant our total attention. We benefit from listening, not only in the information we attain but because it encourages women to continue talking and reveal more about themselves.

I'm not suggesting you never talk. However, silence is advantageous in the following situations:

1. When a woman is talking about an issue that she has a lot to say about.
2. When a woman is getting very emotional about a subject dear to her.
3. If she pauses and looks deep in thought she most likely needs time to think.

Silence allows women time to think. It also encourages them to share more information with us. We need good information in order to understand her at a deeper level. This way we can determine if she is a good match for us and vice versa.

Using silence is smart. Think of it this way: When someone gets arrested, what is the first thing that happens to them? They are read their Miranda warnings. The first of these is, "You have the right to remain silent." Why are these words first? Because when you are silent, you cannot incriminate yourself. Let women express their needs – and, at the same time, don't incriminate yourself. A comfortable silence shows respect to the woman you are with in the aforementioned situations.

Questions and Switching

Now that we know the ideal times to remain silent, what about the other times when there is silence and we become uncomfortable? --During these moments, instead of talking, we should ask good questions or do what's called "switching." Questions and switching keep conversation moving and help us attain more information about the women we are with. In fact, we need to be asking good questions and switching a considerable amount of the time. We should follow up a majority of our responses to a woman's questions with new questions back to her. You can avoid uncomfortable silences and have a lot more success with women when you stop pitching yourself and start switching!

Remember, whenever you are talking, your date cannot talk. Women want to be understood and we cannot understand them when they are not talking. We must be listening. A good formula to follow during a date or interaction is to aim to be listening 65 percent of the time and talking 35 percent. This is an easy formula for you to follow when you are asking enough good questions.

SWITCHING- A Switch occurs when men are talking and we consciously make a shift to focus the conversation back to the woman, where it belongs, by asking her a good question so she can talk and share more information.

Switching allows you the ability to both attain and share information with women in a non-threatening manner. One major benefit of switching is that it helps keep the focus off you and on women and their needs, where it belongs in order for us to have the best success. In one form, switching may be characterized as simply asking extended questions. In another form it can be characterized as your ability to answer questions with questions and to follow up your responses with questions.

When you first meet and begin interacting with a new woman, she is likely going to be somewhat defensive and is not going to be open and honest with her true intentions right at the onset. Women are in protection mode at this stage so they rarely say what they are truly thinking. Why do women act like this? It's a defensive reaction. By not speaking what is actually on their minds, women can gather more information about men before they make a decision. To the vast majority of people, it's much safer to act this way. Covering up what we truly want or feel happens all around us all the time. We often do it too, without even realizing it. I'll give you an example.

Two guys named Bob and Ed are at work in their office one morning. They both happen to be at the water cooler. Bob wants to go to a new restaurant called Height's Cafe to meet a waitress that a mutual friend is willing to set him up with. He wants to see if she is attractive and also doesn't want to eat alone.

Bob: "Hey Ed, I heard from Jim in accounting about that new restaurant, Height's Cafe. Jim said it's amazing."

Ed doesn't want to go out to lunch because he is saving up money for an engagement ring for his girlfriend by packing a lunch and eating at his desk.

Ed: "Jim also told me that it is great restaurant. He said the chicken was fantastic."

Bob thinks he may be able to go to the restaurant but is still not sure.

Bob: "Well, let's check it out for ourselves for lunch sometime. We haven't eaten together in a while now."

Ed: "That's sounds good. Let's get together sometime."

Bob (Now feeling certain and safe): "How about today? We can go get lunch there and catch up."

Ed doesn't want to tell Bob why he is eating at his desk.

Ed: "I can't really eat out today. I have a lot of work to do and am going to eat at my desk."

Bob (Defending himself): "Yeah, I have a ton of work to do myself. Maybe some other time."

In the example above, both men were not really telling the truth about what was on their minds. This happens in most interactions we have with women. It's like having a hidden conversation within the conversation and neither person knows what is truly happening. Why do we act like this? Because it's safe.

Very few people have the ability to be direct and brutally honest about what they really want because they are afraid of what other people will think of them. They don't want to ruffle any feathers, hear the word no or offend anyone. Many women feel it's too dangerous and revealing to speak their minds in a dating situation

Let's look at how this same issue can confuse a good dating situation between Doug and Jamie. Jamie broke up with her last boyfriend because she felt neglected and unappreciated. She felt all he ever wanted to do was sit in front of the television and watch sports at her expense.

Jamie: "Do you like to watch sports on television?"

Doug: "Yeah, I love a good game!"

Jamie: "So you must watch sports on television with your friends all the time?"

Doug: "Yeah, we have a good time. As a matter of fact, my friend, Rick, had us over to his new place yesterday for a baseball game and it was a blast. We spent the whole day over there."

More often than not, Jamie will not tell Doug why she asked him those questions or why she broke up with her last boyfriend. Instead, she will start creating her own internal picture, which may lead her to believe that Doug is similar to her last boyfriend. This very well may lead to her becoming more defensive, concluding that she doesn't want to go out with Doug because she worries she'll be repeating her past mistake. Doug, a good guy, really thinks Jamie is a wonderful woman. He will never know why she didn't want to be with him and never get to know her -- *unless* he stops talking, begins listening and starts "switching" in order to find out the true motivations behind her questions. Doug decided to be too positive and enthusiastic in his response to the sports question, when he would have been wise to find out why she wanted that information by asking a question back to her or switching. Often, when we are too enthusiastic, we end up acting eager at the expense of finding out what the real issue is. Remember, women are a lot like icebergs -- you only see a little piece of them sticking up above the surface. The main parts of their personality and motivations lie beneath the surface.

Whenever we are asked a question, in any circumstance, the woman asking the question wants information for a reason -- even if she is not aware of it at the time. With this in mind, we should strive to know why the question was asked in the first place. Why is she requesting the information from us? What's beneath the surface? We want to know the root cause for the question so we dive deeper beneath the surface by asking questions and switching. Women appreciate this display because it is a quest for knowledge about them, and an attempt to understand them.

Women love to feel understood!!!

What would happen if Doug used the switching technique in the same dating situation?

Jamie: "Do you like to watch sports on television?"

Doug (Switching and more focused on her needs than himself): *"Did you ask me that question because you are a sports fan?"* or *"I like to watch a good game. Do you like to watch sports as well?"*

Jamie: "Not really. It takes up the whole day watching a game."

Doug (Switching): *"I can understand that. May I ask you why sports on TV is of interest to you?"*

Jamie: "It's not really. It's just that my ex-boyfriend would never take me out to dinner because he never wanted to miss a game. I felt like the television was more important to him than I was."

Doug now knows the real issue behind her questions about sports.

Doug: "I am sorry you felt that way and I understand how that could be upsetting. Well, I do like sports but I would certainly rather be out with you."

In that example, Doug switched a couple times to find out exactly why Jamie was asking him the questions about his involvement with watching sports. In this instance, Doug stayed out of trouble with Jamie. And, even more importantly, he understood the one issue that was important to her. Now he knows an important need she has that wasn't met in her last relationship. He understands her better now and she feels more understood. When women feel understood, good things happen!

If you hear a woman say, "Wow, I feel like you really understand me!" that is a very good sign. It's a precursor to intimacy and relationships.

Before we go over the peak times to use switching, we need to talk about three ideas to keep in mind when you are asking a lot of questions and switching.

1. Use complimentary statements that help soften the question or the switch in order to get a candid response. You can create your own that you are most comfortable with but here are some examples:

   That's a great question, You make a wonderful point. Thanks for asking me that. That question must be really meaningful to you. I sense that's important to you

   Woman: "Do you like to watch sports on television?"

   You: "I sense that's important to you. Are you a sports fan?"

2. Make certain your tone is appropriate. Very often men who change their behavior and begin to switch and ask lots of good questions take on an abrasive tone. In extreme cases, this may cause women to not want to answer the question. Keep that in mind and keep your tone soft when asking questions and switching.

3. If a woman asks you an identical question twice, answer it. Don't annoy her. It is unusual that a woman will ask the same questions twice. When women hear the switch, they tend to think that their question was vague and they will usually ask you a different question or make a statement.

Switching happens when you are naturally interested in a woman's needs. With that said, here are some "peak" switching times to become aware of when interacting with women:

1. Transitional questions in normal conversation.
2. Awareness of pressure statements.
3. When insignificant words are used in place of answers.
4. Gut feelings.

Transitional Questions in Normal Conversation

Let's say you are involved in a 10-minute discussion about a subject and all the talk is related to that specific subject, movies, for instance. At some point, your date asks you a totally non-related question to movies such as, "How do you feel about interracial marriages?"

Where did that come from? The point is, there was a reason why she changed the subject just then. Switch and find out why she transitioned the conversation because something triggered her to want that information from you. Find out what it was.

You: "Shawshank Redemption was a fantastic movie. Did you like it?"

Woman: "Yeah, I thought it was great. By the way, how do you feel about interracial marriages?"

You: "You must have asked me that one for a reason." or "I think it's perfectly normal. You must have asked me that one for a reason, though."

Woman: "My sister is engaged to a guy of a different race and it's causing a lot of problems in my family."

You: "How do you feel about it?"

Woman: "It's been difficult for me because I am now serving as the messenger between my sister and my parents."

You: So you feel the pressure of being caught in the middle between your sister and parents?"

Woman: "Yes, it's very draining for me sometimes."

Awareness of Pressure Statements

Sometimes what may seem to be a question is really a statement, knowingly or unknowingly made to put pressure on you. I'll give you an example. A woman says to you, "You know, you always do this to me!" That's not a question, it's a statement and you don't need to answer it although most men do. You need to take the statement and help your date adapt it to a question. For instance:

Woman: "You know, you always do this to me!"

You: "You always do this to me' means?"

To answer the question grants weight to the statement, which may very well put you in a bad position. Always keep in mind that there is a difference between conveying and protesting. Conveying, such as, "You know, you always do this to me!" might be a way your date handles anxiety. It may not be a criticism of you. But you need to find out.

Conveying

Woman: "You know, you always so this to me!"

You: "Which means?"

Woman: "You just are funny that way, that's all."

Protesting your action might mean she wants to talk about making a change. For example:

Protesting

Woman: "You know, you always so this to me!"

You: "Which means?"

Woman: "Which means I would like you to please stop doing that.

You need to find out what your date is thinking by switching.

When Insignificant Words Are Used in Place of Answers.

There are several words in the English language that, when used as answers, really don't mean anything at all. Unfortunately, many men take them as acceptable answers to our questions even though they are designed to confuse and not let us know where we stand. Here is a list of some of these words. Don't use them as answers to women's questions. And don't allow them to be used as answers to your questions. Use switching when you hear these words used as answers.

Ponder, might, maybe, conceivably, perhaps, possible, consider, good chance, look into, try, could be, don't worry about it, sounds good.

Don't guess or assume the meanings of these words. Switch to clarify!

Example 1:

You: "Would you like to get together next weekend?"

Woman: "Maybe."

You: "Maybe means yes...means no...do you have something else planned already?"

Example 2:

You: "Would you like to stop over at my friend's party on Friday night?"

Woman: "I'll consider stopping over."

You: "Great, it would be nice to see you. When you say consider, what do you mean by that?

Example 3:

You: "Will you call me and let me know where you are going to be later tonight?"

Woman: "Sure. I'll try."

You: Cool. When you say that you'll try, are you going to call?"

Example 4:

You: "Would you like go out to dinner with me sometime?"

Woman: "Possibly."

You: "Possibly?"

Woman: Yes, I would like to.

Gut Feelings

If you get a gut feeling that causes you want to want to ask a question, ask it. Trust yourself. It's often the questions that pop up in our mind -- or the ones we don't want to ask because we fear they might make a woman feel uncomfortable – that are the very questions a woman would like to be asked but that, in truth, would really make *us* feel uncomfortable. Find a soft way to ask tough or hard questions by using techniques such as 'a friend' story.

Let's say you get a gut feeling that a woman you are dating is seeing another man but you are uncomfortable asking about it. You could say:

Friend Story

"Maggie, my friend Bob was dating a wonderful woman a few months back and he started feeling really uncomfortable when he sensed she began seeing someone else in addition to him. The two of them had never talked about seeing other people so it left things

81

kind of up in the air. Bob realized this but began feeling really bad about the situation. What's your opinion about that scenario? What would you feel like if that happened here between us?"

Until you feel comfortable openly expressing your feelings, this is a good way to confront what could be a difficult situation.

The bizarre truth about asking tough questions is that we often find ourselves waiting until we have enough comfort and trust established before we ask them. But it is the confidence and emotional intelligence imbedded in the act of asking tough questions that actually can establish trust and comfort in the first place.

Questions sometimes take shape in our heads and we become afraid to ask them. Don't be. As long you learn to ask difficult questions in a nice way and your intentions are good, feel comfortable doing so. We need to be comfortable asking tough questions because it is how we attain quality information about the woman we are with.

A.C.H.I.N.G.

Emotions cause people to take action. People are motivated into action on a pain/pleasure continuum. Pain in your social life is what I describe as *aching*. Many poets and authors have described love as the deepest pain but pain nonetheless. People can go out with someone because they're attracted to them but if you dig a little deeper and ask yourself the question: "What is the motivation behind the attraction?" it leads back to some form of *aching* every time, usually some form of loneliness.

Why would a healthy women go out with a healthy man? Because she is single and her being single at some level serves as a problem to her. Otherwise she wouldn't take the action of going out with him. Healthy people can get to a place in which they are okay being alone but we all know that – for most people -- finding someone you want to be with is preferable to being alone. *Aching* motivates us to do things in our social lives. By tapping into what motivates someone, we are exploring their most basic drives and urges. Therefore if we succeed they feel completely understood.

Have you ever wondered what is the motivating factor or catalyst for a woman deciding to go out with you? Most men assume it's their physical looks or stature. And, in some cases, they may be correct. But even then, the vast majority of time women will decide to go out with you for one main reason. It involves at least one facet of A.C.H.I.N.G. in her social life.

A – Anxieties
C – Critical Problems
H – Hidden Problems
I - Insecurities
N- Negative Feelings
G- Guilt

If you have ever read or studied Greek mythology, you may recall the story of Achilles. He was a fearless warrior and the primary hero in the Trojan War. When Achilles was a baby, his mother, Thetis, attempted to make him invulnerable by dipping him in the river Styx. As she dunked him in the river, she held him by the heel and therefore never got his heel wet with the magical water. This resulted in Achilles becoming immortal except for his heel, where he was as vulnerable as any other human. The vulnerability and weakness of his heel eventually causes his downfall from power.

When we are dating or interacting, it is important that we find a woman's Achilles heal or *aching* in order to cause the downfall of the female guard. This agenda has several benefits. First, you have a goal that takes your mind off sex because if you don't find her *aching*, your chances drastically decrease that you're going to have any intimacy with her. Second, as you will learn later on, finding *aching* is one of the most important avenues you can take to improve your social life and the social life of the woman you are with. It helps you in becoming a more intuitive person who can get to the point, and be honest and direct while deeply understanding women. *The way we find a woman's aching is to ask women questions that allow them to bring up their own problems and become emotionally involved in a discussion with you.* When women are deeply emotionally involved in a discussion, your switches are likely to go unnoticed and there is a better chance that you will hear truthful information.

You must understand that the biggest problem we men face when interacting with women is overcoming their inertia. People by nature are very resistant to change. This is the reason many unhappy couples end up staying together when they should part ways. Two people go out and they move in together or start becoming intimate and it becomes a very comfortable arrangement. Unfortunately, when one or both people in the relationship decide it is time to move on, it becomes an extremely difficult situation because it is tough to give up the comfort of the familiar and risk being alone again. Most people by nature are reluctant to change unless enough *aching* is present to warrant the change.

Now let's take the fact that women are resistant to change. Couple that with the fact that women are naturally attracted to men who are like them. That means if a woman is in a not-so-wonderful relationship and is hesitant to change in the first place, why would she want to go out with you, if chances are that her current boyfriend is probably more or less similar to you in the first place?

If you think about it, when we meet women, most of us become focused on talking about the benefits we can offer her. And at first glance we think it makes sense. Why not talk about what we can offer women? It's impressive if we have nice things to offer that she might like or may benefit her. Maybe it's the fact that we have a good job or a nice car, a lot of money, good connections or come from a wonderful family. Make no mistake about it, those things are all nice to have. There is a major problem with that thinking, though; it rarely leads the woman to change.

What ends up happening is that when we are interacting with women we begin to hear a little "benefit voice" in our head. It says things like, "Somehow, work your new promotion or the fact that you have a brand new car into the conversation; she will like that." And we listen to the voice and think we are moving in the right direction. Let me ask you this. What happens if you feel that you don't have any benefits to offer a particular woman? Many men refer to this scenario as the woman being "out of our league." The same little "benefit voice" we hear has now turned on us and is telling us we are not worthy to be with this particular woman because we have nothing to offer her. Or it might say, "You can talk to her as soon as you have something to benefit her."

Most men like to pitch benefits we can offer but when we don't have any perceived benefits, it puts us at a disadvantage. If we meet a woman that we find truly amazing, we often cannot approach her. And under the "only if we can benefit her theory," it makes for a great excuse not to approach her at all. If we cannot offer her anything to improve her life, it's a great reason not to bother or take the risk. I want to tell you right now that no woman is ever out of your league due to benefits. Ever! And I am going to prove it to you.

First we need to dig a little deeper, though. What actually causes a woman to make a decision to take action or make a change in the first place? We want women to overcome their inertia and take action towards us. If you recall from the earlier chapter on mindset, women in motion remain in motion. Many men fail to realize the simple reality that all women make decisions and take action for two reasons only:

1. To move toward pleasure or happiness in her social life.

2. To move away from pain or *aching* in her social life.

How can we use this simple information to our advantage? By eliciting favorable emotional states through asking good, honest and direct questions. Focusing on how we can convince a woman to go out with us because of the benefits we can offer her is the wrong approach and doesn't lead to actions or change. That would be appealing to her intellect. Although that is what most men do, it's the wrong approach. And even when it works, it's draining!

The exact motive for why a woman will go out with you falls into one the following seven categories of emotions.

1. Present A.C.H.I.N.G. In Her Social Life

Loneliness. Find out if this exists as soon as possible! Ask women questions like: "Are you involved with anyone now?" "Do you have a boyfriend?" "Are you currently seeing anyone?" It's important that we ask women these questions because experiencing and confronting loneliness puts women in a different mental reference when you are speaking with them. When a woman begins to feel *aching* in the present, she is much more likely to want to go out with you.

2. Future A.C.H.I.N.G. in Her Social Life

Fear of the future status of her social life is also a motivator to make a decision but isn't as effective as current *aching*. "Do you ever feel like deep down you're not going to be able to find anyone?" "Do you see your current boyfriend as the ONE for you?" "Do you think this 'being single' thing is ever going to end?"

3. Present Happiness in Her Social Life

This is the woman's longing for pleasure right now. "How much do you wish you had someone to be with now?" "Wouldn't it feel wonderful to have someone to spend time with now and never have to go out to bars like this one?"

4. Future Happiness in Her Social Life

Delayed pleasure is less persuasive than instant pleasure. "Wouldn't it be nice to settle down with someone you feel comfortable with?" Women need some kind of history with you in order for this to be a motivator.

5. Past A.C.H.I.N.G. in Her Social Life.

Women may want to stay away from duplication of an earlier mistake and be looking for certain qualities you possess that a past boyfriend or husband might not have had. "If there was ONE thing that your ex-boyfriend was lacking, what was that?"

6. Past Happiness in Her Social Life

Women may want to revisit past happiness. "What is the one thing that you miss most about your last relationship?"

7. Appeal and Excitement.

These are the flimsiest motivators but the ones many men mistakenly think are most important. "Did I mention I have a Porsche?" "Do you know how many people want to talk with me because I have a lot of money?" "I am exhausted, I get up at 5 a.m. to go to the gym every morning."

Many behavioral psychiatrists agree that the tendency for women to move *away from* immediate *aching* is more of a motivational factor for taking action and making change then is the motivation to move *toward* the promise of happiness in the future. This means that women decide to go on a date, become intimate or get into a relationship with you for emotional reasons mostly related to present *aching* in their social life. Men usually focus directly on the weakest of the emotions, which are Appeal and Excitement. We do this because we are actually trying for a favorable result by tapping a woman's intellect.

Men who attract a lot of women learn and apply a secret that other men never learn or fully understand. *The secret to successful interactions with women is not recalling what to say but rather knowing the right questions to ask, questions that lead women to bring up and reveal their own aching.* I suggest you focus your attention on finding women that have present *aching*. If you meet a woman who has no present *aching*, I suggest you move on to a woman who does.

Unfortunately, many men today become fixated on certain women and waste much time waiting for an opportunity to go out with a particular woman. What are these men doing? Although they don't know it, these men are hanging around like leeches waiting for *aching* to present itself in these women's lives, when there are literally millions of women who have *aching* right now.

Remember, women make dating decisions emotionally...and the strongest emotion is *aching*. Therefore, you might want to choose the most logical and reasonable means for succeeding by pursuing only present *aching*. When you are able to find a woman who feels present *aching* and then demonstrate to her that you are confident and understanding, your social life will begin drastically improving. Keep in mind that while we are not geared to go after *aching* in a way that a trained mental health professional would, we can uncover rudimentary motivational factors.

The following is a sample process to follow when you meet a new woman that you are attracted to and would like to go out with. Remember, you are not trying to make friends with her, you want to go out with her and there's a difference. As we learned before, women find men attractive who are confident and direct in a nurturing way. So go after what you want while softly asking good questions that will reveal her *aching*.

Aching Dialogue

When you come across a woman that you are genuinely attracted to, compliment her with something like," I think you are really attractive." From our section on indifference, we know that women need compliments and it is always okay to compliment a woman you find attractive as long as you really mean it. (Note: Attractive women sometimes complain that they hate it when they are complimented on their physical beauty. If a woman says this to you, know that she is confused or lying. Women need and like compliments. What they hate is when the compliment is insincere. It's always okay to compliment a woman that you find attractive as long as you mean it.) Pause a few seconds and wait for the thank you since this gives her time to take in the compliment. This is one of those good times to remain silent. She should respond with "Thank you" and be a little startled with your confidence and directness.

Then go right for the present *aching*. Get right to the point and ask *her the most important question a single man can ask a woman*: "Do you have a boyfriend?" or the more politically correct version "Are you involved with anyone now?"

If she answers no, this begins to reveal her *aching* in the present. It is absolutely mind-boggling how many single men will meet a woman they are attracted to and not ask this question within the first two minutes, let alone the entire night! The question is so critical and should be asked right at the beginning of an interaction with a woman.

Women who do not have boyfriends or who are not involved with anyone have some degree of present *aching*. Beware: women mislead to protect themselves. Very often when a woman is confronted with the question, "Do you have a boyfriend?" she may lie to protect herself and say a misleading "Yes" in order not to reveal her *aching*. I suggest that you listen with your whole body to her answer. As we continue through this exercise you will learn that even if she is misleading, we will be able to tell and confront her about it.

Women can answer the question, "Do you have a boyfriend?" or "Are you involved with anyone?" in one of four ways:

A: Yes, I do have a boyfriend
B: No, I don't have a boyfriend
C: Some version of, "I am kind of seeing someone" or "I am kind of sort of seeing a couple guys."

D: They will respond back with a question. "Why do you ask?"

Here is how you can reply in each scenario:

A:
Woman: "Yes, I do have a boyfriend."
You: (complimenting her) "He sure is a lucky guy." (Wait for the thank you.) "Let me ask you this. How long have you two been together?"
Woman: "About two years."
Man: "So you must be in love with him?" or "Is he the ONE?"

If the woman you are interacting with answers "Yes" and you believe her, it's time to walk away and move on. You might say:

You: "Well, like I said before, he is a lucky guy and I am happy for you."

Move on because women that are truly in love or have found a man they perceive as the ONE lack present *aching* in their social life and we must respect the fact that they are happy. If the woman answers, "No" or gets quiet and her face starts to wince or says she is not sure, we have to softly dig in at this point.

You (softly): "Well, if you have been with him for two years and you're still not sure if you're in love with him, you're probably not and never will be. Doesn't it make sense to go out with other men to find someone so that you can answer yes to that question without a doubt?"

Or

You (softly): "Did you give up at some point on finding someone you are undoubtedly in love with or do you always settle for mediocrity?"

These are tough questions to ask in this scenario. There is a good chance that the woman will get upset if you ask them. The truth hurts sometimes. If you do sidestep asking these questions, you are not going to have a chance to go out with this woman. Very often these are the tough questions that will jostle a woman to move. So you have to ask yourself a tough question: Is it worth asking a woman a question that might get her upset if it is the only way to have a chance to go out with her? Remember, women who have boyfriends are not moving. The questions above, if asked appropriately, may be the jolt or crash cart to get her moving again.

B:
Woman: "No, I don't have a boyfriend."
Man (setting up for compliment): "Really? I am surprised."
Woman: "Why are you surprised?"
Man (compliment): "Because you are so attractive and so well-spoken that I would think a lot of men would be attracted to you. That's all." (Now become silent and listen very carefully. You are most likely going to get one of two responses.)

1. "Thanks. I just got out of a relationship" or "It's really hard finding a good guy. "
2. Some versions of "All men are terrible." Now it's time for you to go negative or Stay Onsides.

You: "So even if you met a wonderful guy, you probably wouldn't want to go out with anyone?"

Woman: "Well, I never said that. I would want to."

C:

Woman: "I am kind of seeing someone."
You (switch): "That's nice. What does that mean?"
Woman: "Well, I have been seeing this guy and I don't really know what's going on exactly. We are just kind of hanging out."
You (negative or Staying Onsides): "So even though you don't really know what's going on, you probably would be closed-minded to seeing anyone else?"
Woman: "No. I am open to meeting new people."

D:

Woman: "Why do you ask?"
You: "Because I think you are attractive. Are you involved with anyone?" (Repeating your question again and then follow with A, B or C)

While listening for *aching*, it is important that you continue to ask more questions that can expose more *aching* so you can understand the woman even more closely and also employ active listening.

Intellectual vs. Emotional *Aching*

The reason you need to ask more questions while probing for *aching* is that sometimes women deal with *aching* on an intellectual basis. For instance, if you asked:

You: "So how does it feel to be single?"
Woman: "It's difficult, but the odds are good I will find someone eventually."

"It's difficult but the odds are good I will find someone eventually" is an intellectual answer to your question. Women that are expressing emotional *aching* use more emotional words and phrases. For instance, a more emotional response to your question could be:

You: "So how does it feel to be single?"
Woman: "It's so *horrible*" or "I am *worried* I will never find anyone" or "I have *lost all hope*"

Here is an example of how asking more questions can turn intellectual *aching* into emotional *aching*:

You: "So how does it feel to be single?"
Woman: "It's difficult, but the odds are good I will find someone eventually."
You: "There are never times when you feel alone?"
Woman: "Well, sometimes I feel like it's *hopeless and I get down.*"

At this more emotional point, women are more conducive to accepting your invitation to go out then if they are in a purely intellectual state.

Active Listening

At this emotional point, it is important that you do not judge the woman you are with. Instead, become a good listener. Let me suggest some active listening techniques you can use to build trust while listening for *aching*.

1. Women that are discussing *aching* like to know that you comprehend what they are saying. You might want to incorporate the following statements into your vocabulary. You should recite them back when listening to women talk at any time but especially when they are conveying *aching*:

   "That makes sense to me." "I understand." I hear you." " I see what you are saying." and "I think a lot of people feel the way you do."

It's amazing that simply expressing that you comprehend and understand what women are saying helps to build so much trust!

2. Reiterate what the woman you are with is saying or feeling when she expresses *aching*. It's very soothing for women to feel like they are being comprehended and understood, especially when they are emotional. A good way to convey your understanding is to repeat the words or emotions of what was just said.

Repeating Words:

Woman: "All I wanted was to do something nice for him and he threw it back in my face."
You: "You wanted to do something nice and it was thrown back in your face."

Repeating Emotions:

Woman: "It hurt so much when I felt like I was second in line to the television on Sunday. I was so frustrated and upset that all I wanted to do was take a sledge hammer to the television and start World War Three."
You: "It hurt and you felt frustrated and upset."

3. Make an analogy or summarize what a woman has just expressed to you:

Woman: "The situation left me no choice other than to leave. I did everything I could do."
You: "It looks like you came to the end of your rope."

Here are some phrases you can use when you feel sure you understand what was just conveyed to you:

"From your perspective..."
"You feel that you..."
"I hear you say that that you felt like..."
"I get the feeling that you..."
"It looks like you're saying that..."
"It feels like you..."

If you feel uncertain that you understand what the woman is communicating, you can use these phrases:

"I may be way off base here, but I get the feeling that you..."
"Could it be possible that you..."
"Just to see if I hear what you are saying correctly..."
"If we are on the same wavelength, I am hearing that..."
"I think what you're saying is that you..."

These past sections exemplify how you can take charge and steer a conversation towards *aching*. Finding out what a woman does for a living, where she lives, if she's having a good time tonight, etc., should all come after first finding out if she has any present *aching*. It's important that you adopt this strategy and do not gauge the success of your social life by benefits that you can offer women. Instead, learn to ask questions geared at finding *aching*, and listen for *aching* clues and cues when women are talking.

If you decide to spend two hours at a party talking with an attractive woman and fail to ask questions that uncover that she is moving in with her boyfriend of three years (a guy she's madly in love with), then you have just missed countless opportunities to talk with other women. Please be good to yourself and seek out women with *aching*. Your time and happiness are important. It's also important to realize that women make decisions to go out with you or to become intimate with you based on their own *aching*. Many men are afraid to take risks and ask women out because they feel they might be rejected.

Know that you don't have to feel vulnerable anymore because now you understand that women make decisions based on their own aching. In many cases, their availability to go out with you has nothing really to do with you at all!

Whether you go out with a woman or not, like many things in life, is often a matter of *timing* more than anything else. Do they have any *aching* at the time you want to ask them out? Do you?

8

Concept 5: Intimacy and Sexual Guilt
Quantifying and The Kiss of Death

Where is Your Date 0-10?

Many men find it difficult at the end of a date to gauge the extent to which the woman you're with had a good time or not. What we actually want is some sort of feedback as to what she is feeling in regard to her interest in you. If you feel confused as to whether or not the woman you are with had a good time then you can use the female scale of interest to help women put a numeric value on her feelings at the end of an evening.

Female Scale of Interest

-Negative- 0-1-2-3-4-5-6-7-8-9-10 *+Positive+*

At the end of the night, it could sound something like this:

"Jenny, let me ask you a question. On a scale of zero to ten, zero meaning that you had an awful time tonight and never want to see me again and 10 meaning you had an amazing time tonight and would be open to going out again, where are you?"

Listen closely. Your date will be conveying her interest level in you. If she says 10, you know that you have a woman who is really interested and it's most likely safe to initiate physical contact. If she says anything less than a seven, she probably didn't have that good of a time and felt the two of you were not a good match. Initiating physical contact in this situation may not be wise. If you get less than a seven, tell her nicely that you don't understand why she said that. Listen carefully to her response; she will most likely reveal more *aching* about her social life at this point, more of what she needs that she is not getting. Can you fill that need? Do you want to? Or is it time to move on?

You most likely will hear women rate their night somewhere between seven (7) and nine (9). To which you respond: "Jenny, what would it take for you to get to a ten?" Many women at this point will actually ask you to kiss them or invite you in. The statement, "Jenny, what would it take for you to get to a ten?" is actually a very nice compliment. So at the end of a date I would suggest the following:

If you get a 7 to 10, it's safe to assume that the woman had a nice time and has a relatively high interest level in you. You have a high degree of likelihood that an initiation of physical contact by you will be accepted and that she will want to go out with you again. If you get less than 7, I suggest you first ask why she felt that way. Then, if need be, go negative with something like, "So you probably don't want to go out again?" If she doesn't become more positive it just might be time to move on.

As dating is certainly not an exact science (and we wouldn't want that to be the case), you can use the 0 to 10 technique as a way to help relieve some pressure and gauge more closely what your date is feeling in quantifiable terms.

Don't Be Like Other Men and Ask Women To Have Sex. Be Different and Have Patience -- *They* Will Ask *You!*

Women are, by and large, much smarter than men due to a greater degree of emotional intelligence. If you think for a second that the woman you're dating doesn't realize that you are male and want to become intimate with her, then you're living in a dream world. While it is okay for men to take the initial steps to initiate intimacy (hooking up), if you Stay Onsides, women will eventually ask you to have sex with them.

While hooking up with women, be different from most men. Don't pressure women for sex. Instead, ask a soft question like, "What do you want to do now?" When you ask soft questions like that, it places all the decision-making power on the woman -- where it belongs in the first place. Let her retain her decision-making power. It's her place to decide when and if she wants to have sex. If you allow her to keep her natural power, she most likely will want to, it's just a matter of time. This also builds trust since the woman cannot accuse you of pressuring or forcing her to do anything she wasn't ready for.

If a woman asks you back, "Do you want to have sex?" I suggest you answer it truthfully. A good response would be: "Yes and No."

You could say:

"I do think you're a beautiful woman and I am really attracted to you, so yes, I sure do. But only if you feel that you are ready. If you are not ready, I would have to say no, I wouldn't want to do something you are not ready for."

With that statement, you state the obvious and convey that you are attracted to and care for the woman you are with. You also show that you care for her well-being. This reply also keeps you Onsides.

Sexual Guilt

Does anything feel better than when you first become intimate or begin forming a meaningful relationship with a woman you are fond of? You have applied your attitude and mindset, trust-building tools, set a solid Opening "No" Agreement, listened, asked good questions, and found *aching* in a way that the woman felt understood. Now the woman wants to become intimate with you.

At this point, men are taught to jump right into physical mode and not say a word that could ruin this wonderful situation we now find ourselves in. We attack physical intimacy like a starving animal attacks food. Many men believe that you have to act swiftly in this situation or the opportunity will vanish.

Not so fast...

We need to be patient. Many women suffer from something called sexual guilt that can kill and/or mortally wound relationships. What usually happens is that men who are shy or aggressively flawed are so frustrated at interacting with women that when the opportunity of becoming intimate presents itself, they feel that it's like a lunar eclipse -- only available for viewing now and again. If they don't hurry up and get out their telescope, it will be gone and the show will be over. They feel they'll have to wait another four years to have another chance.

These men have been convincing instead of leading, preaching their benefits instead of finding aching, and talking instead of listening all night long. They believe this window of opportunity is going to close very soon so they need to "get her" very quickly before she comes to her senses or the alcohol wears off, whichever comes first. They don't want this golden opportunity to be squandered so they become pushy and want to act fast.

Often, women who become intimate with men second-guess their very personal sexual decisions. They have thoughts like: "Did I become intimate too fast?" "This guy must think I am sleazy now!" "I put myself in such a vulnerable position and have no control now!" Women who feel they were manipulated or pressured into intimacy will generally want to make some sort of attempt to regain control of the dating process. This usually sounds something like, "I want to slow things down" or "Let's take a break." It's the kiss of death for a relationship.

For men who genuinely want to begin building a relationship, sexual guilt represents a large problem. These problems often begin by having a face-to-face talk or receiving a phone call in which the woman is backing out of a mutual relationship-forming process. By wanting to "slow things down" or "have some time apart" women are saying that they want to be in control instead of having a balanced relationship dynamic. It's a symptom of sexual guilt rearing its ugly head.

While nothing feels as good as sex, nothing feels quite as bad as having a small taste of intimacy with a women that you would like to be with, only to have her cut off the intimate relationship for unknown reasons until she feels it's time to continue again (if she ever does). This controlling behavior by women puts us in quite a precarious position. We have no idea where we stand anymore. In order to continue the relationship, we must assume a subservient role in which we are not getting our needs met. It's an adversarial power shift and it's the final part of the woman's system we need to learn to overcome.

When a woman says, "Let's slow things down" or "Let's take a break" she is telling you that she wants to be in control of the relationship because she feels vulnerable or afraid. Switch and find out what her statement, "Let's slow things down" or "Let's take a break" means to her. Most often, it will mean you will have to let her be in control and you be subservient to her if you want to have your needs met. Part of her being in control is doling out how, what, when and where you will be getting your needs met. Women use this behavior as a last-ditch effort to protect themselves from men.

What we can do is alleviate sexual guilt from destroying or interfering with our relationships. As a matter of fact, we have been doing most of the work all along.

If you have learned and used the concepts taught in this book so far, the woman you were with felt in control from the moment you met her.

- She decided whether or not to go out with you.
- There was never any negative pressure applied to her.
- She decided whether or not to continue going out with you and had the right to say "No" at any time without feeling bad about herself.
- She possesses and has always possessed decision-making power
- She had no need to try to disappear from you

Caution: Even women that have this much freedom still can catch a nasty case of sexual guilt! Good news, though. There is something we can do about it. Like a flu shot, we can expose women to a small dose of sexual guilt while they are still in our presence and deal with it before it grows into a full-blown epidemic affecting our relationship.

Before getting into an intimate situation, here is what you do:

Bradley Fenton

When a woman asks you to have sex with her, purposely bring up sexual guilt before you have sex for the first time. It sounds something like this:

"Meredith, I really think that you are beautiful and I want you to know that I don't want to do anything before you are ready or before you feel comfortable. How are you feeling?"

Continue.

"I want you to know that if we have sex, I think it would be wonderful. I know that some women, after they have sex, feel sometimes like things moved too fast and they may want to take a break or slow things down. Now, I care about you and would rather that we waited longer to have sex if you are going to feel like that afterwards. I bring this up because I don't want to get a phone call later saying that you want to slow things down or things are moving too fast and you want to take a break. If that's the case, I would rather we just waited."

It's important to give women the opportunity to back out from first-time intimacy they might not be ready for if you want to form a meaningful relationship with fewer problems. Women will almost always agree to continue anyway, but if she is feeling uncomfortable about something, now is the time to find out while you can still talk about it without abusing her trust.

Even if she suffers from some sexual guilt when you're not present, the fact that you were willing to postpone intimacy will become instrumental in her not wanting slow things down. She begins to think, "Maybe this relationship is going too fast and I need some time to slow things down...But I already told him that I wouldn't do that to him. And besides, he is a good guy and I trust him. He wouldn't even sleep with me until he made sure I was ready."

If women want to slow things down or take a break, find out what that means exactly, by switching. Most often, it is not okay, as relationships move backwards only at someone's expense. In fact, I suggest in most instances it's time for you to end the relationship with her. Remember that women say this usually out of fear because they want to be in control. We cannot have a balanced and equal relationship when a woman wants to be in control at your expense. If you hear, "Let's slow things down," and you see no reason to do that, I suggest in most cases you need to end the relationship. Women have to choose: it's either you or their fear.

Bradley Fenton

9

Concept 6: Roadblocks to Your Success
They May Not Be Your Fault But May Be Your Problem

Have you ever wondered why some men can approach women and strike up a conversation while others cannot take the risk? We all want to be able to walk up to and begin conversing with new women we find attractive but in reality very few men actually possess this ability. What is it that makes up the subtle difference between a man who can take that risk and one who cannot?

I want you to know that you can become a man who is able to walk up to women you find attractive -- if you choose to be. First, you have to overcome some roadblocks. While they can all be overcome, it is not an overnight process. To accomplish this, you will need an open mind, a forgiving heart and a sincere and patient dedication to achieving the confidence needed to do what you really want.

Roadblock #1: Personal Warning Beliefs

Dating and interacting with women is a self-fulfilling prophecy or what's known as the Pygmalion Effect. This means that you are going to cause women to behave in a way that is in harmony with how you yourself would behave in a similar circumstance or how you would truly *expect* women to behave in that situation.

106

A great example of the Pygmalion Effect comes from George Bernard Shaw's play, "Pygmalion." The central character, Professor Henry Higgins, asserts that with dynamic training he can transform a Cockney flower girl (considered to be low class) into what society perceives as a high-class duchess. While he succeeds at his task, his trainee, Eliza Doolittle, makes a crucial statement in regards to the idea of the self-fulfilling prophecy while talking to a friend of the professor's named Pickering. She says:

"You see, really and truly, apart from the things anyone can pick up (the right clothes, the correct speech, etc.), the difference between a lady and a flower girl is not how she behaves but how she's treated. I shall always be a flower girl to Professor Higgins because he always treats me as a flower girl, and always will but I know I can be a lady to you because you always treat me as a lady and always will."

Eliza Doolittle makes a good point that also rings true for single men. We teach women how to treat us from our early interactions with them. If we set a faulty dynamic upfront, problems will persist. In addition, if incongruence between how we feel we deserve to be treated and how we are actually being treated appears it causes a problem, which sends us a warning and leads us to take action in an effort to receive a different outcome in a similar situation in the future.

While growing up, many men have unknowingly created personal warning beliefs. Men create these beliefs starting in childhood as a form of protection and often carry them into adulthood, where they have a tendency to become faulty and cause problems. We weigh these internal beliefs in interactions, where they help us determine how to behave and make up our expectations of how we are supposed to be treated. Here is an example of the forming of a personal warning belief by a man named James. James grew up in a family in which he was continually told that under no circumstances could he talk to strangers. In one particular instance, at the age of five, he was waiting for his parents in the lobby of a fabric store while they were shopping for curtains. He was bored and began talking with a store clerk about baseball. She took a liking to him and offered him some juice and cookies in the store cafeteria while he waited. James wanted the juice and cookies and accepted her offer.

According to James, when his parents returned from shopping, they were frantic to find him. After a couple of very anxious minutes, it was pointed out to them that he was having a snack in the cafeteria. Frightened by a rash of child abductions in the area, his parents scolded and punished James for talking with a stranger, let alone accepting juice and cookies from someone he didn't know. James was made to promise that he would never again talk to strangers.

Right or wrong, James learned from very early on that it was not okay to talk with strangers. This personal warning belief was formed in order to protect him during his childhood years. The problem is, nobody ever told James when it was time to discard that belief. Moreover, most men are not even conscious that they still are carrying these beliefs around in their heads. Like shedding dead skin so new skin can grow, many beliefs from childhood should be discarded or changed as one transitions into adulthood. Sometimes, men unknowingly hang on to some outdated beliefs that worked very well during childhood but are harmful to them during their adult years.

Fast-forward 30 years. The adult-and-single James is at a party and sees a woman that he finds to be attractive. He wants to walk over to her but just cannot take action and doesn't really understand why.

As he begins to force himself into action, he gets a strong signal blocker to stop that behavior and instead never takes the chance. He doesn't realize what stopped him from doing what he wanted. All he knows is that he cannot do what he wants and it lowers his self-esteem.

The woman at the party was a stranger to James. And "It's not okay to talk with strangers" was one personal warning belief that James had unknowingly held onto since childhood. He would have chosen to discard this belief earlier if he could. But the problem was he was not conscious that it was there in the first place. This is an example of just one of hundreds of potential signal blockers that may be impeding you from doing what you really want.

Here is a list of some common faulty personal warning beliefs or expectations that appear most often and that I consider to be hindering single men:

1. I must pretend to ignore women I am attracted to.
2. I cannot tell a woman I find attractive that she is attractive to her face.
3. It's not okay to compliment women that I find attractive.
4. I can't ask a woman out when I first meet her.
5. It's not okay to fail.
6. It's important women like me.
7. It's not okay to talk with strangers.
8. It's not good to analyze my interactions.
9. It's impolite to ask women if they are involved with anyone during our first conversation.
10. It's impolite to ask women how long they have been with their boyfriend in our first conversation.
11. It's impolite to ask women if they are in love with anyone during our first conversation.
12. It's okay if a woman I am dating wants to slow things down.

13. I must act tough to women and act like I am playing it cool.
14. Most women are truthful when I first meet them.
15. I can't ask women out unless I am wealthy.
16. I am not good-looking enough.
17. I can't confront women.
18. I can't ask a question that might cause a woman to become upset.
19. "No" is not an okay answer.
20. I need to lie to women to make myself look better.
21. Women that give me their phone number are just being nice and don't really want me to call them.
22. Some women are out of my league.
23. I have to date women my parents would like.
24. I must date women that would impress my friends.
25. I don't have much to offer women.
26. Sex is an immoral act.
27. Women don't find me attractive.
28. Other men deserve to be with women more than I do.
29. I am going to have nothing to say and it's going to be awkward when I approach women.
30. Silence is uncomfortable.
31. Most women are attracted to very muscular men.
32. It's normal to go for months without a date.
33. Women that are negative are the hardest to talk with.
34. Women that are very positive are the easiest to date.
35. It's hard to meet women where I live.
36. I don't have time to meet women.
37. If I am right and a woman is wrong I must correct her.

38. I don't like walking up to women I don't already know.
39. I must talk a lot to keep the conversation going.
40. I am not happy with myself.
41. It's rude to ask women a lot of questions.
42. Women like men who talk a lot.
43. If a woman has a boyfriend I can't go out with her.
44. It takes a long time to meet women.
45. There are certain things that you just can't say.
46. Some women are really difficult to talk with.
47. Some of this book doesn't apply to me.
48. I must find out about a woman's past before I can go out with her.
49. My time is not valuable.
50. I like to think things over before I decide to take action.
51. I don't deserve to be happy.
52. I need to act perfect around women.
53. Dating isn't fun.
54. I am uncomfortable with certain aspects of dating.
55. It matters what women that I don't know say, do or think about me.
56. I am very different than most men.

Faulty personal warning beliefs are often the source of excuses not to take action. They hinder men from reaching their desired outcomes with women they would otherwise choose to be with. If any of your personal warning beliefs contradict your preferred outcomes or anything we have learned so far in this book, then you are going to shy away from something you know would be in your own best interest.

Take note of the personal warning beliefs that may be disrupting you from achieving the results you want. Then follow these steps:

1. For each faulty personal warning belief that you possess, question yourself as to what kind of effect you're getting as a consequence.

Example:

Personal Warning Belief: It's impolite to ask women if they are involved with anyone during our first conversation.

Effect: I often spend large amounts of time talking with and buying drinks for women that are involved and in love with other men.   It results in frustrating evenings in which I meet no women to go out with.

2. Decide how you would like your results to change.

I would like to find out at the beginning of an interaction if the woman is involved and/or in love with anyone else, so I can determine if it makes sense to continue talking to her.

3. Change the personal warning belief into a supporting belief that will take you to your desired outcome.   Rewrite your faulty personal warning beliefs into signal supporters or positive affirmations that begin with: I *must*, I *choose to*, I *can*, I *have*, I *am*, I *will*, or I *do*.

Example:

Supporting Belief – I must ask women if they are involved with anyone early on during our first conversation.

4. You have a couple of ways to internalize these signal supporters. You can choose to recite these signal supporters aloud every morning as you awaken and every night before you go

to sleep. Or get a tape recorder and fill up both sides of a blank tape with your own voice reciting these signal supporters repeatedly. Then play the tape several times a day. When you reach a point that these signal supporters become imbedded in your subconscious and second nature, you have successfully overcome the first obstacle.

Roadblock#2: Identity

I will begin discussing the Identity Roadblock by introducing a hypothetical situation. Imagine you are walking down the street on your way to work or school and suddenly a car pulls up. Two men in dark suits and sunglasses grab you and knock you unconscious, then toss you inside their car and whisk you away. You awaken to find yourself in a magnificent, spacious room with no doors or windows. The only thing inside it is you and the comfortable hammock you are lying on. You are frightened because there is seemingly no way out. But you also feel oddly at ease because the room has such a relaxing and calm aura, almost as if it were tailor-made for you. Suddenly, a hologram appears in the room. The hologram is a man wearing a tuxedo suit with a top hat. He looks like he is either going to a fancy wedding or is some kind of a magician. You wonder what in the world is happening.

He says, "My name is Mussewbee" and he asks you, "How are you feeling?" You demand to know what is going on, where you are and why you were kidnapped (expected questions for this sort of scenario!). He answers, "I will explain everything" and asks you again, "How are you feeling?" Instead of arguing, you find yourself answering, "I am oddly feeling wonderful." You listen as he tells you that this is your new home. He explains further that after his first visit with you, no other person or hologram is ever allowed into this room. It's all yours. He then goes onto say, "When you are in this room, you are no longer any of the characters you play to anyone else in the outside world." Still confused, you ask what he means by characters.

Mussewbee says, "You are no longer a worker, a student, a bachelor, a computer wiz, a golfer, an athlete, a friend and so on. None of that exists here in this room. It's just you and your hammock. That's all."

Let's pause the story for a second. What if you were stripped of all the characters you play in your real life today? Your job is gone, you are not a buddy to your friends and all your characters have been taken away from you. Grade yourself, with one (1) being the lowest grade and five (5) the highest. What grade do you give yourself without any of the characters you play in your life? Circle a score on the rating card below on how you feel as a person in society with no characters to play.

Rating Card

Lowest 1-2-3-4-5 **Highest**

Now back to the story.

Mussewbee continues, "This room is located deep inside the core of the earth. It was a gift to you and you alone, in which to relax and find peace. A special hard drive has been implanted in your head, which allows you to come and go from the room as you please. All you have to do is close your eyes, take three deep breaths and you will be transported right into the room where you will find yourself lying in your hammock with the same relaxed, comfortable feeling that you feel right now. When you want to go back to the outside world, close your eyes and go through the same breathing ritual and you will be back. It's that simple." Then the hologram vanishes. You close your eyes, take three deep breaths and find yourself back on your walk to work, just like you had been before this had ever happened. But from now on, you are free to visit and leave this room for the rest of your life, whenever or wherever you please. It is your safe haven.

Now that the story is finished, let's take a look how you rated yourself on the rating card without all the characters that you play in your life. Without these characters, you are left with your identity. If the grade is anything less than a five (5), you will have extreme trouble taking the risks needed to meet new women. Knowing that you are always at least a five (5) is one of the keys that confident men hold. They can detach themselves from certain situations that would seem uncomfortable to them otherwise. How can they do this? Because no matter what the outcome of the interaction with a particular woman, they know that they have no control over her final decision. And they always have that relaxing room to go back to. Their identity is strong enough to buffer them from the negativity and discomfort that a negative result might produce because they have let it go and feel comfortable waiting for the result in their private rooms. In fact, we all have this safe haven or safety net available to us. But many men rarely notice it is there. Finding access to your identity leads you to the important realization that:

It doesn't matter what anyone says, does or thinks about you. It only matters how you feel about yourself.

Most men have never been taught that how you feel about yourself means more to you and your success with women than anything else. Therefore, they rate themselves less than the top score of five (5).

Many men say things like, "Those characters I play are so vital and make me who I am today."

The reason I used the private room example is that people are a lot like that private room deep inside the core of the earth. Other people encircle us, yet we live in our own worlds, within our own rooms, within our own bodies, within our own minds. We were born into the world alone and that is the way we are going to leave it. If you have ever had surgery, you may understand what I am talking about. When the general anesthetic kicks in, you realize that it's you who are going to sleep and nobody else. It can be a very overwhelming feeling.

We were born into this world without any characters to play. A little baby boy isn't supposed to do anything but eat, sleep, and excrete. All of the characters that you play in your life exist in order to fit in with society. Consequently, you have the ability to separate yourself from these characters, if need be. It's important to always have respect for both your personhood and that of other people, while realizing that there is a difference between the characters we play and our identity or true selves. Simply having this realization is one of the factors that will get us closer to where we need to be for more success with women.

You are *not* what a particular woman at a party thinks of you. You are *not* what you do for a living and you certainly are *not* the car you drive. Our society lends itself to men believing that the characters we play define who we are. Think about the invisible lines we create. How many times have you seen an attractive woman and assumed that a woman like that would only go for a powerful professional like a business executive or surgeon? When you have these thoughts it very well might be that your identity is not as strong as it could be. Much of this stems from our childhood.

Many men are taught from a very early age that how well the characters we play in society will determine our value as a person. Our parents, teachers and other authority figures told us that good elementary school scores would get us into the top high school classes, and top high school classes along with good grades would determine the college we attended, which in turn would determine what kind of job we would get. And what kind of job we got would determine if we were successful or not. And that kind of success was the measure of our value as a man. In other words, climbing each mountain would lead to climbing another mountain and then another. There would be no time for stopping or resting. If we did, our fellow mountain climbers would pass us by and that would be tragic.

Consequently, many men in our society are poisoned into believing that success is determined externally rather than internally. Learning to feel good about yourself was irrelevant because it was society's opinion of you that really counted. In other words, what happens in the "real" world creates what life is like inside us, internally. Gentlemen, if you learn anything by reading this book, understand that just the opposite is true.

From the privacy of our very real, private rooms, we can create the external world.

Remember your authority figures saying things to you like:

"Did you do all your homework?"
"So-and-so got a great job, what are you doing?"

In order to answer these questions confidently and remain in a favorable light with your authority figures, many men had to have accomplished something externally. On the other hand, how often

117

Bradley Fenton

did you hear from your authority figures, "We love you for being yourself?"

Men that didn't hear nurturing compliments often have difficulty interacting with women later on in their life. If you heard this said to you while growing up, consider yourself very lucky. Most men are rarely afforded this nurturing, which is unfortunate because it is the emphasis on nurturing and feeling good about yourself, that truly leads a young man to happiness and accomplishment. Unfortunately, our society emphasizes external achievement over internal success. Most people fail to even slightly consider the state your identity is in as you grow up. You could be the nastiest and most miserable little bastard in the world but in our society, if you have straight A's, then you are a prince headed for success. And it continues as you grow. You can be a real son-of-a-bitch but if you have millions of dollars then you are well respected and envied by most people. It's sad.

Growing up, many men were made to believe that we were valued more if we achieved something. And if we failed, we were made to believe we were valued less. Eventually, many men misguidedly believed that character failure was akin to identity failure. *As long as you are truly doing the best you know how at the characters you play, any sort of failure doesn't affect your worth as a human being.*

Do you see abstractly the importance between the characters you play and your identity, and the difference between the two? It makes an enormous difference in how you interact with women. Men always interact with women in line with their internal views of themselves. If a man is having the kind of success with women that surpasses his internal view of himself, he will self-sabotage in order to return to a more comfortable status quo. If you don't learn how to feel really good about yourself, it's very difficult for women to feel good about you either -- or for you to

118

have any continued success for a sustained period of time. I suggest you start working toward building a solid identity.

Roadblock #3: Need for Approval

Need for Approval is another roadblock, like Identity, that comes, once again, courtesy of our society. Estimates show that nearly 80 percent of men suffer from this problem. When it is compounded with the identity issues that we discussed earlier, your life with women will surely suffer. You will not be able to ask them out or get what you want. In addition, you will not be able to act natural in a dating setting. The date or interaction will become too pressure- packed and stressful for you.

Let's think back to childhood again. You were encouraged to make friends and to play nicely with the other kids, weren't you? Then you were encouraged to and probably wanted to become popular in your school. You wanted to make friends and be liked and accepted. Most young people do. In the working world, it is important for your co-workers, bosses and clients to like you. This generates a mindset in men that it is very important to be well-liked by all people, including women that we are dating.

The need for approval from women means that deep down, your need for women to like you will take precedence over a woman respecting you or having an intimate relationship with you. When this happens in a dating situation, it's not really dating. Instead, you have acquired what we call a "very expensive friend." This is the reason for the popular catch phrase, "Nice Guys Finish Last." Nice guys finish last for a reason. The reason is their need for approval and its precursor, identity problems. Men who suffer from not being able to overcome this roadblock are blocked off from being confident. The result is women are much less inclined to be attracted to you.

Need for approval will cause you numerous problems while dating. By far, the four most serious of these problems are the inability to ask tough questions, confront, initiate physical relationships when the opportunity arises and say or hear the word no.

By my estimates, nearly 35 percent of start-up relationships end too quickly due to men's need for approval. Many problems occur early in a relationship, yet men often sidestep tough and uncomfortable questions that we know we need to ask because we fear we could appear inappropriate or might risk the woman becoming upset with us. Men with need for approval can ask regular, run-of-the-mill questions with no problem. What I am talking about are the questions that we are afraid to ask, questions that get to the heart of the matter, like asking a woman you are attracted to if she is involved with anyone upon meeting her.

Many men have occupations that require the confidence to ask tough questions. One man who is an extremely prominent divorce lawyer boasts that he starts off his new client meetings with one simple question, "So who was fucking whom?" Now that's a tough question and he has no problem asking it. Yet this same man, because of his strong need for approval when it comes to women, was unable to get down to the *aching* issues involving his dating life. It took him eight months to be able to consistently ask women he was attracted to if they had a boyfriend when he met them for the first time.

You cannot ask questions that get to the point or heart of the matter when you suffer from need for approval. You cannot do it because there is a chance that a woman would get upset with you and walk away. Remember, dating is a self-fulfilling prophecy. If you do not have the healthy indifference mindset, which allows you to walk away from a woman if you decide she is not right for you, you in turn will not be able to act naturally because her walking away from you would be too devastating and might crush your fragile identity. You couldn't understand her walking away because you couldn't ever do it yourself.

Like we learned earlier, women lie and mislead to protect themselves. Many unsuspecting men have a naïve view of this. So often we are not aware that the lying is taking place. Assuming that we identify the lies, the situation could call for confrontation, which many men cannot accomplish because they worry that the woman will get upset with them. If a woman is lying to you, it should be known that there could never be any meaningful flow of communication or a relationship if you avoid confronting her.

Men with need for approval have a very difficult time confronting women. Confrontation does not have to be a horrible, dish-throwing encounter. Most of the time it is bearable. Men who want to be more successful with women need to learn to confront women in very soft ways. Learn how to confront by first asking a soft question like, "Can we please talk about something without you getting angry or defensive?"

The capacity to initiate physical intimacy when the opportunity presents itself is vital when you are dating. Women sense the lack of courage in men that have confidence issues when it comes to intimacy. Men who have trouble with need for approval will surely understand what a nervous, awkward and terrible time it is not being able to make your move.

Most men with need for approval like people in general. This love of people often is displayed by having good qualities, good interpersonal skills and the realization that they are a really nice person or have the "gift of gab." It is not unusual for them to hear just how nice they are after their first attempt at physical contact and it sounds something like this, "Bill, you are really a special person and such a super guy and any girl would be lucky to be with you, but I am not ready for this. I guess I just don't deserve you."

This really nice compliment will usually be the zinger that Bill loves because in essence he gets what he really wants. Remember, men with the need for approval want women to like them more than they need physical interaction or respect. And that's just what Bill got here. The fact that she complimented him and likes him blinded him to what was really happening. She was ending any chance at a relationship. Women are wonderful at making a huge compliment followed by their strategic rejection. Bob got to hear how the woman really liked him so he will not say anything at his point. He is swimming in the compliment. He doesn't put any pressure back on her. Not figuring out why she just in essence rejected him (although he doesn't realize it yet), there is no way he can have a relationship with her without confrontation at this point.

When you suffer from need for approval, it is very easy for women to take advantage of you. Your inability to say "no" often translates into you doing something that steers you away from taking care of your own needs. When you have trouble saying no, you probably can't stand to hear the word no from women either. This will lead you into big trouble.

Men become wide open to indecisive women leading them on for long periods of time. The reason is because men are afraid to know where they stand because getting to that point may mean it's time to walk away from a relationship or move on. Men with need for approval cannot do this and certainly cannot hear this said to them by a woman they are with.

In addition, remember Staying Onsides? You will never be able to use its powerful effectiveness when you cannot hear or say no. The whole point of that technique is to be patient enough to lead the women to persuade you on why the two of you should be together. When you Stay Onsides, you intuitively let women make their own decisions. Women have the right to decide to say no or end the relationship with you, if they so desire. By giving them that freedom, they are much more likely to say yes. Although using this technique will help you hear yes more often, you have to respect that sometimes you may have to accept a sincere no that might mean the relationship is done. You need to pick up and move on. Conducting yourself in a fashion that is in harmony with hearing no as an acceptable answer is difficult, if not impossible, for men with need for approval.

Regrettably, a vast majority of single men suffer from a high need for approval. For most single men, approval is attained in the form of intimacy with women. Consequently, men continue to do or say anything possible to become intimate and always wing it, even if it means lying. And when they have an intimate experience, even if it has been for the first time in months or years, it's enough reinforcement to continue their faulty behavior.

It's easy during the few days of bliss following intimacy with a new woman to forget that you are unhappy with your social life 99 percent of the rest of the time. This is where men get reinforcement to repeat the behavior that has been getting them such poor results. Like treats to a dog, intimacy is doled out in little portions and they will do whatever is necessary to get it again. It's a vicious cycle caused by a severe ego block. The only way men can get past the block is to believe it's okay for us to accept a no from a woman (that she has that right) and for us to accept our failure and learn from the results.

Sometimes we are afraid of what we don't understand and so it is with failure. We need to understand that men who are afraid to take action with women and risk failure and rejection are also afraid to succeed. Men who have the highest success rate with women and are happiest with their social lives fail at a much higher rate than men who have low success rates and are unhappy with their social lives. One of the main keys to success with women is to be okay with your own failure or what is referred to as "feedback." It's perfectly okay to fail.

Since we are not playing any games with women, our risk and action-taking is in itself winning. We continue to build our self-esteem in the risks and action we take, not the decisions that women make. We do this because we believe that if we continue to take action and risks we will eventually find what we are looking for. It is the ability to take risks and action that allows us to win, not whether a woman decides to accept our invitation to go out or not. That will always remain an unknown.

The only way we lose is by failing to take action at all.

It's strange but you learn a lot more from the failure/feedback (they are really the same word) of hearing a "No" than you do by hearing a "Yes." With this in mind, you can switch your mental goal with women from hearing a "Yes, I would love to go out with you" to having the goal of hearing "No, I won't go out with you." This way you win every time you lose and when you lose, you win big.

Within this mindset is the willingness to hear the word no and overcome your need for approval. Sometimes no really means no, and we must have the ability and courage to walk away and move on, realizing that there are many other single women out there just waiting to say yes. We just need to be in the right mental frame of mind.

Roadblock #4: Tactile Needs and Energy

Men that have strong signal supporters, solid identities and have overcome the need for approval can be thrown off balance by what is believed to be a craving for sex. Some women say it makes us act irrational. It's not really the craving for sex that causes us to act irrational. In fact it's only a small part of it.

Think of the need for sex as an ever-burning match. Now think of the basic need to be non-sexually touched by other beings, like hugging, as one of many gasolines or fuels needed for our body and mind to function correctly. When men neglect our need for non-sexual physical touching, it's like throwing the lit match into the pool of gasoline. It creates an exaggerated burning inferno of need for sex. What's really causing the problem, though, isn't the need for sex. It's the lack of non-sexual and nurturing physical contact like hugging.

Although it may sound cliché, many psychologists agree that a grown man needs four hugs a day for survival, eight hugs a day for maintenance and twelve hugs a day for growth. I am not talking about the superficial hugging or pecking on the cheek that occurs at parties. That's what is called social hugging and it doesn't fulfill the need.

Recall the last time you hugged somebody or somebody hugged you. For most single men, it's been too long. The tactile sense has been documented to be an enormous determinant in child development and happiness in adulthood. In fact, babies initially recognize their parents by touch. Tactile sense is a major factor in developing security and self-esteem and it is a need that we continue to have throughout our lives.

If you're a single man living alone or constantly working, how are you going to have this tactile need met? If you don't get it met at home and certainly not at work, then where? The ultimate in tactile experience is sex.

With that said, many men who do not get enough tactile stimulation, be it sexual or non-sexual, start getting into a rut in which they are deficient in tactile stimulation. It's analogous to being in serious financial debt. So for a man who is at a tactile deficit, having sex is like winning the lottery! Unfortunately, when you're at a tactile deficit, your chances of having sex are only slightly better than winning the lottery. The reason is because when you are at a tactile deficit you begin to "hard sell" women on why they should want to be with you, instead of leading them. You become a poor car salesman out of your neediness. And as we learned, this type of behavior exemplifies neediness instead of confidence. Women are not inclined to be attracted to needy men.

So what can we do about getting our tactile non-sexual needs met so we can be more intuitive with women, leading us to get our sexual needs met? Some men turn to strip clubs or hookers to find this tactile stimulation of energy. But you are not going to find it there. Humans all have a limited amount of energy we can give. Most hookers and strippers have very limited energy to begin with and are running on empty because so many men are taking the little energy they have left to give.

Do yourself a favor and get a pet that you can hug. Believe it or not, it will drastically improve your social life. You can meet your minimum non-sexual tactile needs through hugging animals like a dog or cat (and also give an animal in need a good home). Not only will you have more opportunities to meet women when you are walking a dog, for instance, but having your non-sexual tactile needs met will actually decrease your neediness for sex. It will eliminate the gasoline that magnifies the sex need into a burning inferno and will keep it at a more manageable level so you can keep your wits about you and act intuitively with women.

10
A Parting Thought

Guys, it is very possible in this lifetime to have more happiness with your social life than you ever dreamed of.

It makes total sense to concentrate on understanding women's needs and helping them find a good match, whether it is you or someone else. The more we focus on helping women get their needs met, the more we will get our needs met. With the growing demands of work on your time and a climbing average age at marriage, men who adopt this philosophy will be fortunate while those who don't will be left behind to cope with their frustration and loneliness. The positive and negative lasting effects derived from this choice on both men and women are enormous.

Men who develop higher levels of emotional intelligence and confidence will be able to relate to the women they are with on a much deeper level than ever before. Men who continue to shy away from interactions with women or become overly aggressive will find themselves getting untruthful information and a general feeling of being worn out trying to find a meaningful relationship.

Please practice and review the concepts in this book and assimilate them. Then let yourself go and have fun improving your social life.

LaVergne, TN USA
10 March 2010
175609LV00004B/11/P